How to make
Ceramic Character Dolls
and their accessories

How to make
Ceramic
Character Dolls
and their accessories

Sylvia Becker

SEARCH PRESS

Contents

Introduction

A doll should not only be looked upon as a toy but as something very personal and special. Collecting old dolls has become a popular hobby today, but making your own original doll can give tremendous pleasure and is a means of creative fulfilment.

This book is intended to be more than just an instructional manual. It will introduce you to a whole world of dolls of all types and sizes, ranging from dolls of yesterday to modern models of today. It gives a brief history of character dolls, then goes on to explain with step-by-step instructions and illustrations how you can make your own doll from a specially prepared clay which can be moulded into shape and baked in a normal oven. An alternative method is also given, using porcelain which is not a natural clay but a liquid dough, mainly composed of kaolin and petuntse, and which needs to be fired in a special oven. Both materials have a translucent appearance when they have been fired.

Of course, manufactured dolls may appear more technically accurate but as they are mass-produced they all look alike, whereas a handmade doll is unique and has its own individual character. It is not only the result of your skill and imagination but it will also reflect your personality. You will naturally feel proud when you have created your own doll, but the main enjoyment lies not so much with the finished model as in the hours of pleasure when you were lost to time and surroundings, and completely forgot yourself in your hobby.

If you have long wanted to make your own doll, it is the aim of this book to help you succeed. If the idea has only just occurred to you, then it will introduce you to a fascinating and rewarding new craft.

Sylvia Becker

History of dolls

Everything created by human hands is not only a reflection of its creator but also an expression of the taste and preferences of society in any given period. The same is true of dolls! Even in prehistoric graves we find dolls made of wood, bone or bronze, representing the earliest imitations of human beings. At that time they were mostly used for cultic and religious purposes and dolls as playthings only came into fashion much later, in medieval Europe, where the skilled doll makers who carved dolls out of wood enjoyed great popularity. In Germany, Berchtesgaden, Oberammergau, the South Tyrolean Grödnertal and Nuremberg in particular, developed into early toy-making centres.

Dolls played an important part in recording our earliest history, and they were fashioned from all types of materials, such as wood, wax, porcelain and celluloid, and had many different functions. Today, these dolls have become valuable and beautiful witnesses to the past.

Antique dolls

In France, from the beginning until the end of the eighteenth century, dolls were made from wood and wax, and were intended as artistic and expensive toys for adults. Collectors today regard these as 'fashion dolls', as they were popular with high-society ladies, and acted as mannequins. In this way the newest fashion creations from the noble houses became known, even in distant provinces, and fashion dolls were used in Paris until the end of the Second World War.

In 1805 the doll manufacturer, Müller, introduced papier mâché into his toy production and the doll with a papier mâché head and leather or linen body replaced the wooden doll. However, this material was not very durable and today dolls with papier mâché heads are very rarely found in collections.

Porcelain dolls

Developing industrialization in the nineteenth century made more efficient doll production possible. Between 1830 and 1840 most dolls were produced with glazed porcelain heads, or heads made from matt, marble-like, white Parian porcelain. These cool ladylike models were not the cuddly toys we know today and, naturally, did not endear themselves to the hearts of children. Around 1860, a doll whose whole body was made out of porcelain came on to the market, and these were popular as 'bath toys'. They were mostly made from white glazed porcelain and were moulded in one piece with black, or occasionally blonde, hair painted on, in place of a wig. A doll of this type was known as a 'frozen Charlotte' or 'frozen Charlie'.

In the second half of the nineteenth century, instead of using white porcelain heads, more and more dolls came to be made of flesh-tinted biscuit porcelain and in Sonneberg in 1880, closing eyes were used for the first time. Around this time the doll manufacturer, Heinrich Stier, also developed the doll's body made of linked balls. From the end of the nineteenth century into the 1920s,

French model doll. Wax body with modelled head and real hair wig. Paris c.1784, Victoria and Albert Museum, London.

German doll manufacture developed enormously in Waltershausen and Sonneberg in the Thüringen Forest, and also around Nuremberg. It became a veritable boom and many fine examples from this period still exist today.

Early working conditions

Important manufacturers during this period in Germany were, among others, J. D. Kestner, Kämmer and Reinhardt, Simon and Halbig, Armand Marseille, Ernst Heubach and the brothers Heubach, C. and O. Dressel, Heinrich Handwerk and Bruno Schmidt. Among all these well-known names, the most popular model produced was the Armand Marseille doll with the serial number 390, which was still being produced in 1938.

Unfortunately, the boom also had its dark side because most of the doll production was undertaken by homeworkers, who were very badly paid. For many families, however, this was the only possible way of earning a living and children had to make their contribution as well. Thus it was that dolls designed for the enjoyment of children were produced by other children's hard labour.

French dolls

The doll industry also developed in France during the nineteenth century. Antique French dolls are distinguished by their especially finely modelled heads, beautiful glass eyes and luxurious clothes. On these models the heads were usually made from very fine biscuit porcelain. The best known French doll manufacturer was Emile Jumeau and this firm won medals for their work at every world exhibition in the nineteenth century. Jumeau founded the French doll manufacturing firm in 1843 and even in 1894 was still rightly calling himself 'le Roi des Poupées', 'the Doll King'.

The doll makers from Germany then took over the world market again and in order still to be able to compete, the French companies joined together in 1899 to form the 'Société Française de la Fabrication des Bébés et Jouets' (SFBJ). Members of this Society were Fleischmann and Bloedel, Pintel and Goldchaux, Genty, Girard, Remignard, Gobert, Gaultier and Jumeau. For economic reasons, until the beginning of the First World War, dolls' heads were produced in Thüringen from original French designs, but after the First World War, the French doll-making industry became independent again. Other French doll makers with a worldwide reputation were Casimir Bru, Ferdinand Gaultier, Nicolas Steiner and the Société Steiner and even today, the name Gaultier is well known in the fashion world.

Two French child dolls with biscuit porcelain heads, movable wooden bodies and original clothing. The doll on the left dates from 1896; the one on the right is probably from Jumeau's workshop, Paris 1884, total height 43cm (17¼in), Bethnal Green Museum, London.

Character dolls

'My Darling Baby', Character series 126, Simon & Halbig. Original condition, with hand knitted cap (1910), silver rattle (1920), new dress made from old material and crochet.

The popular Käthe Kruse dolls (left to right): unnamed doll (c.1926), 'Schielböckchen' (1930) and 'Niddy' (1929), all in original clothes. Käthe Kruse Doll Museum, Den Helder.

The educational reform movements of the nineteenth century also had an effect on toys. In 1908, a Munich arts and crafts exhibition displayed a large number of natural looking dolls for the first time. The portrait painter, Marion Kaulitz, was especially successful with her colourful 'doll children' mostly dressed in Bavarian costume. The wooden heads of these dolls were sculpted by Paul Vogelsang and this was the birth of what are now termed 'character dolls'.

Artistic dolls

At first, the efforts of the young Munich artists did not attract much response from the industry, but some manufacturers realized that these artistic dolls embodied ideas which possibly catered for new tastes. The firm Kämmer and Reinhardt did not hesitate for long and they soon launched the first mass-produced character doll on the market, which was called the 'Kaiser baby' with the serial number 100.

Sales were very successful and further character dolls were produced. These are still admired by collectors today and command high prices. Examples include serial numbers 117 and 114, sold as a pair, and also known as 'Hansel and Gretel'. Other large manufacturers followed suit and launched their own character dolls on the market. These included Armand Marseille's 'Dream Baby', Kestner's 'Bye-lo-Baby' and the 'Hilda' doll, produced both by Kestner and Armand Marseille. Of all the dolls produced about this time, however, the firm Kämmer and Reinhardt's number 126, called 'Mein Liebling' was the best seller in the character series.

The character dolls also included the famous 'Googlies' and the 'Kewpies'. Googlies were produced from 1911 and were mainly small dolls, pop-eyed and with mischievous smiles. Kewpies owed their being to the American, Rose O'Neill, and they originally appeared as drawings in the children's stories, 'The Light of the World'. From 1912

Googlies and Kewpies are among the most popular character dolls. Here they are positioned around an interesting old example of a doll's bed. Typical of the Googlies are their cheeky smile and their big wide eyes.

onwards they appeared as dolls, manufactured by the firm of Kestner from pattern drawings. They were produced in all sizes from 2 to 22cm (¾ to 8¾ in) in porcelain and celluloid.

Käthe Kruse dolls

At the beginning of the twentieth century, quite by accident, an unforgettable range of children's dolls was created, known as the 'Käthe Kruse' dolls. Käthe Kruse's daughter wanted a doll but not just any doll – she wanted an original doll to cherish. Käthe Kruse, who was living in Ascona at the time, wrote to Max Kruse in

Berlin, asking him to purchase the most beautiful doll he could find. His reply reads 'I'm not buying you any dolls. I find them revolting. Make one yourself.' (From 'The Experimental Period', by Max Kruse, published in 1983.) She accepted the challenge and in 1905 produced her first doll creation. By 1910 her dolls were on display in the Tietz Store in Berlin and for decades she fulfilled the dreams of many small girls.

Modern dolls

After the First World War there was a general decline in the doll-making

industry. At first, very simple dolls were available on the market with articulated bodies and biscuit porcelain, or hard rubber heads. Celluloid dolls also appeared but by the beginning of the Second World War, the great period in the German doll-making industry was over. After the war some firms began production again and in the 1950s dolls were being made from synthetic materials, with closing eyes, automatic speech and stylable hair.

Celluloid dolls

Some popular Schildkröt dolls (left to right): Bärbel, Inge, Ursel, all dating from the period after the Second World War. The largest seated doll has the serial number 1728/8, (Schildkröt and Kämmer & Reinhardt).

These models played an important part in the development of doll production. The oldest German celluloid factory was founded in Mannheim-Neckerau in 1873 by Friedrich Bensinger, H. L. Hehenemser and Sons and the brothers Lenel. In the 1880s the manufacture of raw celluloid material began but five years later, after a fire had completely destroyed the headquarters, it was decided to change the firm's name and it became known as the 'Rhineland Rubber and Celluloid Factory'.

In 1889 the trade mark 'Schildkröt' (tortoise) was introduced but nobody knows why this was chosen. Perhaps this mark was inspired by the tortoise's strong shell which would have been a desirable quality to attribute to this new material. It was also a selling point to stress that celluloid had the same

hygienic features as porcelain, with the overwhelming advantage of being unbreakable, in fact, as durable as a tortoise's shell.

At the turn of the century 'Schildkröt' had a monopoly in celluloid and it was only produced and sold by this factory. The company not only produced finished dolls but also the raw material, and parts of dolls, to sell to other firms. Among those it supplied were Kämmer and Reinhardt, J. D. Kestner, Koenig and Wernicke, as well as Buschow and Beck in Nosen. In 1903 there was a break with the latter firm, when it became known that they had started their own production of celluloid goods, but Buschow and Beck survived the ensuing economic crisis without too much hardship.

Over the decades, countless doll models were introduced by the

Rhineland Rubber and Celluloid Factory, but it would take too long here to give full details. Among those produced after the Second World War the best known were probably 'Hans', 'Christel', 'Bärbel', 'Inge' and the very popular 'Strampelchen'.

Today, dolls in all price ranges are to be found in toy shops, doll boutiques, department stores and even in mail order catalogues. Old-fashioned porcelain dolls are reproduced and modern versions of artistic dolls, now manufactured in vinyl, are obtainable at attractive prices. Old dolls for collectors and handmade artistic dolls are sold at auctions and special sales and fetch very high prices. Perhaps, one day, your own unique original doll will also become a treasured heirloom.

Group with a nostalgic air (left to right): standing front AM 370, sitting AM 3 200 with leather body in original condition, right AM 390. Back row: standing 'Mein Goldherz', Bruno Schmidt, original condition new clothes; sitting doll, probably French, original clothes.

Workshop

In this book we show you how to make two different types of doll, one fashioned from a modelling clay and one from porcelain. The basic principles for making both kinds of doll will be explained in the following pages.

In doll making, nature remains the best teacher, and observation is an important factor. As the creator, however, you have the freedom to stress particular features. It does not matter in the least if the head of a child's doll is a bit too large or the hands and feet a little too small; it emphasizes their likeness to children. Similarly, it can enhance the effect to make the limbs of a fantasy doll grotesquely long.

Nevertheless, although the reflection of human characteristics must be taken into account, dolls must still remain dolls!

Anatomy

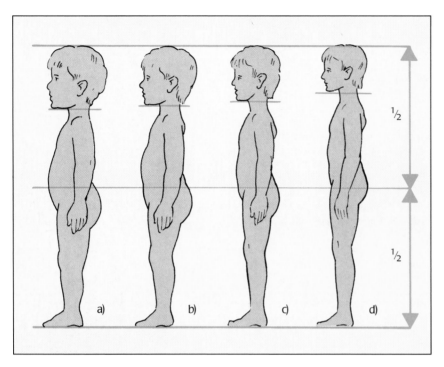

The relation between the head size and total body length changes during growth; a) at 2 years, b) at 3 years, c) at 5 years, d) at 7–8 years.

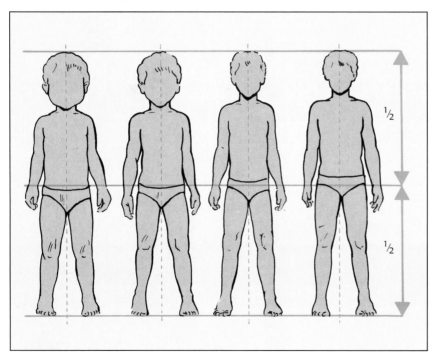

The relation of arm and leg length to the rest of the body also changes during growth. The hip line gradually rises to about the centre of the body.

The ratio in the size of different parts of the body to one another is fundamental in making a doll. The most important relationship to establish is that between the size of the head and the length of the body. In a small child of about two years of age, the whole torso length amounts to about four times the length of the head, whereas with an adult it is seven times. The arm and leg proportions also alter as we grow up and when a small child raises its arms they only just meet above its head, whereas in adults, the crook of the elbows reach that far.

As a general rule, with growth the hip line gradually becomes the centre point of the body's total height; arm and hand together are as long as a leg; the elbow is the centre point between the shoulder and hand joint, and the knee is central between the hip-joint and the sole of the foot.

Head and face

A child's head, as well as its body, changes as it grows. As a baby the face is soft and round but as it develops, the features become more marked. For example, a baby's nose is small and snub and the bridge of the nose is flat. As the child grows older its nose becomes longer and narrower. A child's nostrils are round, whereas an adult's are oval-shaped. A child's chin is recessive and roundish, but in a grown-up person it is more prominent.

The position of the eyes also has a strong effect on facial expression. If you draw a line through the middle of a face, a small child's eyes lie below it, whereas a grown-up person's are above this line. Further details about the proportions of head and face will be examined when dealing with modelling.

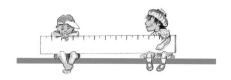

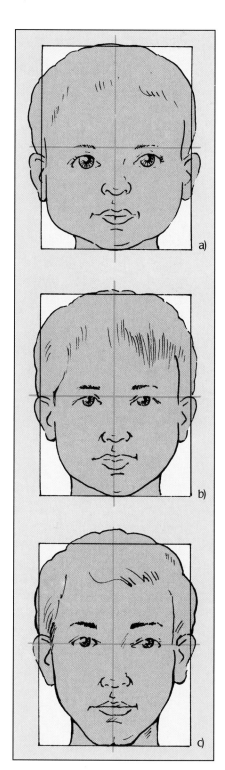

Hand and fingers

The hand is one of the most complicated parts of the human body. Look at your own hand and compare it with the diagram on the right.

On average, the middle finger of an adult hand is as long as the palm of the hand, that is, the length from the wrist to the beginning of the fingers. As a rule, the thumb reaches to the second joint of the index finger and is about as thick as the middle finger. If you point your thumb outwards, then the palm of the hand becomes a square but the palm and fingers together make the hand rectangular.

Seen from the back the fingers appear flat, but viewed sideways all the sections of the finger are slightly rounded. One section is about a third of the whole finger in length. As a guide, the whole length of a human hand reaches from about the chin to midway up the forehead.

Foot and toes

On average, the adult foot is as long as the whole human face. The toe joints are shorter than the finger joints, and except for the big toe, much smaller. The top of the foot slopes slightly outwards and the toes also point outwards a little. Each of the small toes has three joints, the big toe, however, only has two. The inner ankle is higher than the outer ankle, and the heel looks like a triangle, going from the sole of the foot to the top of the ankle.

Obviously, a child's hands and feet are substantially smaller than those of an adult.

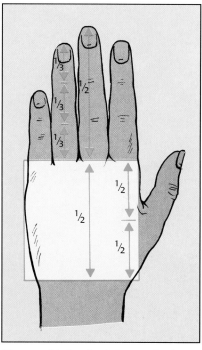

Diagram of the hand with finger and palm proportions.

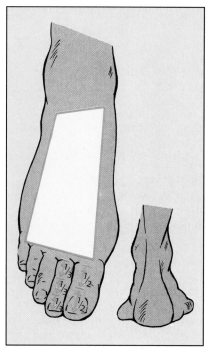

Diagram of the foot showing proportions of toes, top of the foot and heel.

The eyeline in a) a baby, b) child aged 4–8, c) an older child.

Materials and tools

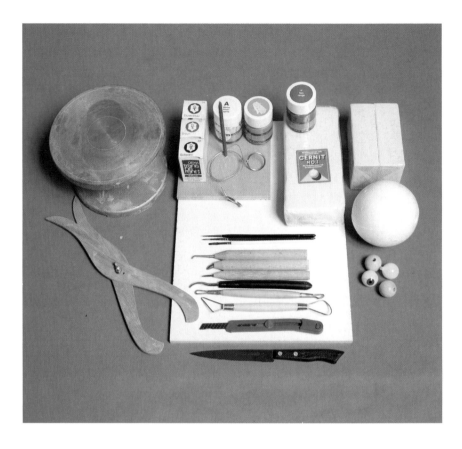

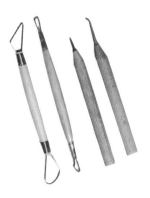

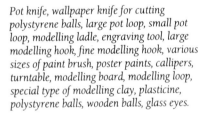

*Pot knife, wallpaper knife for cutting
polystyrene balls, large pot loop, small pot
loop, modelling ladle, engraving tool, large
modelling hook, fine modelling hook, various
sizes of paint brush, poster paints, callipers,
turntable, modelling board, modelling loop,
special type of modelling clay, plasticine,
polystyrene balls, wooden balls, glass eyes.*

Working with modelling clay has an
advantage over porcelain as it is less
time-consuming, however, each doll is
an original model. This type of clay is
an art material and it is possible to roll
and shape it directly from your
preliminary model. To make a
porcelain doll, however, an
intermediate stage is necessary, and
from the original plasticine model a
'negative' must be prepared which can
be used again and again.

Modelling clay

If you do not wish to go to the expense
of buying, or hiring, a suitable oven for
firing porcelain, you can obtain a
special clay which can be moulded into
shape and baked in a normal kitchen
oven. When baked it becomes
translucent and looks like porcelain. It
comes in various colours and can be

obtained from craft shops, or shops
which specialize in doll-making
materials and equipment. It is
important to note that a normal
oven-baked modelling clay will not
have this translucent appearance. The
manufacturer's catalogue clearly states
the purposes for which it is intended
and the required firing temperatures,
and this should be kept for reference.

This material is ideal for rolling out
and shaping. It does not dry out and
can, therefore, be worked with over a
long period of time. Even after fairly
long pauses in your work, you can join
new parts to parts you have already
prepared. It is also used by
professional doll makers for their own
creations.

Plasticine

Plasticine has a great advantage over

any other material which can be used
to make the original model, as it does
not have to be prepared. If you work
with clay or plaster, it is necessary to
prepare the model with shellac
beforehand. If you use plasticine, this
stage can be omitted and you can take
the mould directly from the model.

As plasticine remains pliable while
you are working it, this means there is
no problem if, when you are making
the mould, small overlaps occur and
you need to take your model out of the
plaster to correct them, see pages 28
and 29. Like modelling clay, plasticine
does not go hard and this gives you
plenty of time to work on your model.
It can also be reused, so you do not
have to buy new materials for every
new design.

Scalpel, round scalpel, cow hair brush, fine and coarse engraving tools, hole cutter, scraper, fine cow hair brush, eyeballs, goat hair brush, synthetic brush, separator, porcelain dish, sponge, metal corner, mould tin.

Porcelain

Biscuit, or unglazed porcelain, is the traditional material used for making dolls. T
made f
feldspa
ready
purcha
differe
or brov
is pour
negativ
very qu
from th
few mi
the inn
porcela
the por
poured
porcela
surface
(fractic
remain

mould to dry until it becomes leathery, then the mould can be opened. This porcelain blank must dry out
e it is
elain is fired
from 1,190
°F).

urntable,
k at your
ost common
is that they
n the front
inate
happen
es much
e front.
modelling
cting the
delling
ing out the

clay and to remove the model from the turntable, and pot loops and modelling ladles for shaping. All of these tools can be purchased in a craft shop. To begin with you can make do with knitting needles, pin-heads, toothpicks and teaspoons as additional tools.

To make a mould and work on a porcelain blank, you also need extra implements. You will require a mould tin, a metal corner, plaster, clay and porcelain dough. To carry out the work you need to use a sponge, a scalpel, eyeballs, scraper and brush. If you do not have your own oven suitable for firing porcelain, ask about the possibilities of hiring one in your neighbourhood. Further details will be given in the ensuing chapters.

Shaping the basic model

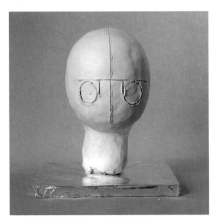

Precisely mark the eye height, distance between the eyes and their circumference.

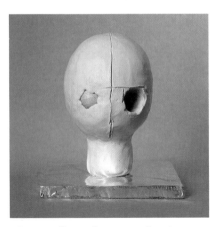

Dig out sufficient plasticine to allow the eyeballs to fit easily into the holes.

Position some plasticine to indicate the nose.

Base the modelling and sizing on a child of about six years of age. Don't be shocked by the size of the model, as the end product in porcelain shrinks in baking and is about 30 per cent smaller than the model. When it is finished the doll will be about 46 to 50cm (18 to 19¾ in) long. Begin by setting out a square board, into which you have knocked a 15cm (6in) ordinary nail, then cover the board with aluminium foil.

Modelling with plasticine

For the head you will need a total of about 1,200 to 1,400gm (42½ to 49½ oz) plasticine, and two wooden balls for the eyes about 2cm (¾ in) in diameter. First make a ball with 800gm (28¼ oz) plasticine, which you have rolled out. For the neck make a roll 5cm (2in) long out of 130gm (4½ oz) plasticine. Press the neck roll on to the nail, place the head on top of it and in order to get the proportions right for the face, draw a central vertical and horizontal line on the front of the head. A small child's eyes are set under the horizontal line and the distance between the eyes is about the same size as a single eye. To position the eyes put one of the two wooden balls on the cross between the two centre lines and on the left and right of the ball, draw in the distance to the eyes. From these two markings you can draw in the position for each eye, both placed under the horizontal centre line. With the modelling loop remove enough plasticine from the two eye sockets to enable the balls to fit in neatly. Now smooth round the edges of the balls with a little plasticine.

Form the sides of the nostrils with small balls of plasticine.

In a baby, the cheeks extend under the chin.

Form the upper lip and the chin and position the lower lip under the upper lip.

With your finger and thumb pinch a little plasticine between the eyes, just below them, to mark the nose and add a bit more plasticine to form the nose. For the outer edges of the nostrils make tiny holes with knitting needles. When you are modelling the cheeks, eyebrows, ears or other parts of the face, make a plasticine ball for each area and cut it in half to ensure that both are the same size. Make the chin from a small halved ball.

Let the upper lip protrude slightly and the lower lip reach up to it from underneath. A child's mouth points distinctly upwards and the lower lip is shorter than the upper lip. Lower eyelids and brow are formed in the shape of a stretched out plasticine bead.

Smooth the plasticine down and look at the face sideways. Take the head off the board and alter it as necessary and round off the neck at the bottom, so that later on it will fit neatly into the breastplate, then put the head back on.

For the eyelids 2mm (¹⁄₁₆ in) thick rolls are used and pressed firmly in place. To model the ears turn the head sideways and draw a vertical line from the lower jaw and an oval sloping towards the back of the head. To ensure that they are the same size, fix the position of the top and bottom of the ears with toothpicks. For moulding a porcelain head, see pages 28–30.

As a basic rule use the same amount of plasticine for each limb. Estimate about 250gm (9¾ oz) per leg and 80gm (2¾ oz) per foot; 100gm (3½ oz) per arm and 40gm (1½ oz) for each hand.

Position the eyebrows with a roll of stretched out plasticine.

After every step, smooth over the head again.

To form the forehead, add some plasticine and smooth it down.

Looked at from above, the forehead looks narrower than the back of the head.

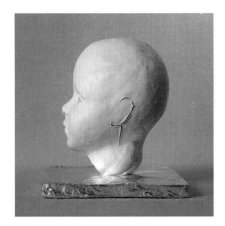

Position the ears sloping slightly towards the back of the head.

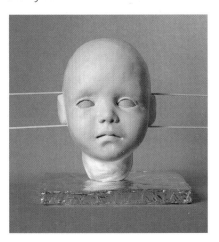

Use toothpicks stuck into the plasticine to check whether the ears are set correctly.

Modelling with clay

When you begin working with oven-baked clay, make sure your work surfaces and hands are very clean, or you may discolour the clay. Do not wear dark woollen garments, as it is difficult to remove threads which may stick to the clay.

As a general rule the baking time for this type of clay depends on the thickness and size of the part but it should be hardened in a pre-heated oven at 102 to 133°C (215 to 270°F) for between 5 to 45 minutes. Do not exceed the maximum recommended temperature. During this period the material becomes quite soft and it is necessary to support delicate sections. If a crack develops during baking, it can be filled later and baked again, and any excess clay can be sanded or filed down. During the baking process the clay takes on a translucent appearance.

Colouring the clay

This material is available in many colours but if you use number 1, which is white, it needs to be tinted. It is best to do this a few hours before you begin modelling. The clay becomes quite soft when it is kneaded and should be allowed to stand in a cool place.

To colour the clay before baking, use poster paints but be careful not to make the flesh tints too pale. Mix ochre with a little white and a trace of vermilion in a dish, then with your fingertips spread a little colour on to the clay and knead it in thoroughly. Repeat the process until you achieve the shade you want. Make sure it is coloured all through and that no stripes or smears of colour remain.

To paint the clay when it has been baked, use water-based or acrylic paints. Do not use oil-based paints without first applying a foundation, see page 36. Before colouring, wash each part with detergent and water. After painting, a varnish may be applied, but do not use spray or metal lacquers, or nail varnish, as these have an adverse effect on the material.

Clay head

Take about 700 to 800gm (24¾ to 28¼ oz) of clay and so that it does not become too heavy, insert a polystyrene core. For this you need a ball with a diameter of 8 to 10cm (3¼ to 4in). Cut it to the right and left and hollow out the front. This hollow is then packed with modelling dough, so that the eyes may be set in later. When this is done, cover the whole face area with clay 1cm (½ in) thick. Stroke the joins carefully with a modelling spoon and then flatten with the fingertips. You now have an oval, which looks rounded from the side.

Hold the head firmly by the still unused piece of polystyrene as you need to apply some pressure to set in the eyes. As with the plasticine head, draw a vertical and horizontal centre line to ascertain the height and distance of the eyes. With a pointed knife or the modelling loop make two hollows for the eye sockets.

Setting in the eyes

To set the eyes in, either make two balls out of uncoloured white modelling clay or use glass eyes. Note that eyes made of any synthetic material are not suitable because the head will have to be hardened in the oven. Eyes made of clay have to be painted, but you are saved this task if you use glass eyes from the beginning.

Place a clay base on the modelling board to serve as a neck and then put the head you have modelled on top of it. Now work on the back of the head and begin modelling the face. This is done in the same order as for the plasticine head.

Finally, form the ears because after baking you can no longer work the modelling clay. Details for working the outer shape of the ears are given on page 35. When you feel satisfied with the results, look at your work critically once more from all sides, then take the head off the board and round off the bottom of the neck. For baking put the head back on the modelling board. Pre-heat the oven and bake your model two or three times for twenty minutes at about 110°C (230°F).

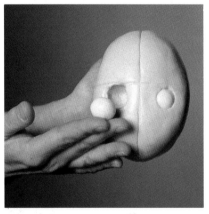

Fill a polystyrene ball, which has its front side cut off, with modelling clay.

Draw the guide-lines and make the eye sockets.

Set the head on the neck and join them together.

Head of a doll made from oven-baked modelling clay. Anna has green eyes and long shining reddish hair. This is matched by the delicate green dress and a large ornamental lace collar. The straw bonnet adds the finishing touch.

Modelling with clay

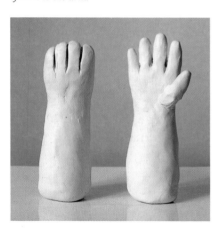

Model the right-angled shape for the hand and join it to the arm.

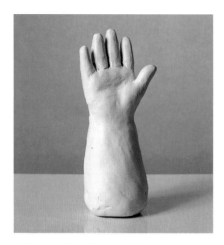

Cut out the fingers and add the thumb.

Hollow out the palm of each hand in the centre.

Modelling arms and legs

When modelling arms and legs always work each pair step-by-step at the same time, so that you obtain equal results. Before you begin, check the section on anatomy again, see pages 16–17, and note the details for hands and feet. For each limb, make a roll that tapers towards the end. At the narrow end, the corresponding hand or foot is shaped.

Cut in for the fingers and toes with a knife and round them off with a modelling ladle. Model the thumb separately and attach it to the palm of the hand. This also gives you the ball of the thumb. To work the surface of the hands and feet, also the instep and heel, use the pot loop. In modelling the hands and feet, material is removed rather than added. Once you have completed the modelling, set the hands and feet in the required position but make the doll's posture look natural.

As with the head, to avoid too much weight insert a length of electric flex about 1.5cm (⅝ in) diameter. Cut a piece of flex for each limb and draw out one of the wires from the flex. This is necessary so that you can insert a knitting needle into it later, to use as a

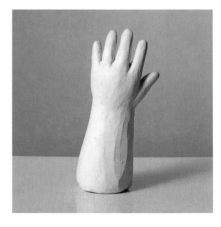

Corresponding to the curve of the palm, flatten the outside of the hand outwards.

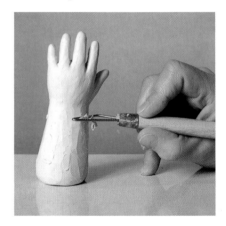

Make the wrist a bit narrower with a modelling loop.

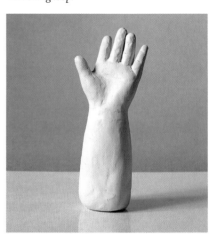

Place the modelled hand and the individual fingers in the required position.

Join the foot, which looks like the sole of a shoe, to the leg.

holder. Form a roll of clay round the flex you have prepared in this way. The flex should still be visible at the top end.

Before you begin any modelling detail, stick the limb on a knitting needle, which has been run through the flex. Hold the needle with your left hand, while you work with your right hand. This will ensure that you do not spoil any parts you have finished modelling when you pick it up or put it down. For casting arms and legs in porcelain, see page 31.

Supporting device

If you bake the arms and legs by simply laying them on a baking tin, you could get pressure marks on the back. You therefore need to prepare a supporting device for when you put the limbs down or when you bake them. To do this, take a ceramic pot – a flower pot is best – and half fill it with stones. This ensures that the weight of the limbs will not tip the pot over. Cover the top half of the pot with crushed aluminium foil, then stick the knitting needles into the foil. For modelling arms and legs in oven-baked clay, follow the same instructions as given for the basic model.

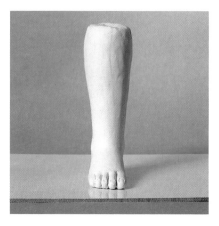

Round off the toes upwards and downwards. Draw the nails.

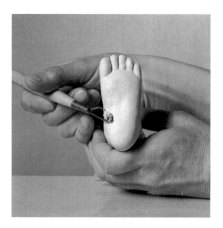

Hollow out the middle of the foot. Form the heel and the ball of the foot.

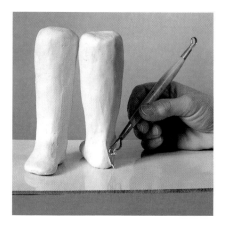

Flatten the instep at the toes and dig out the heel.

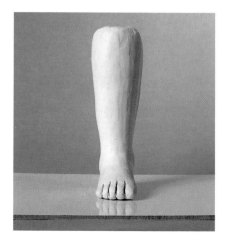

Cut out the spaces between the individual toes.

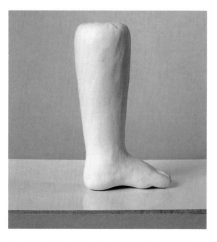

Looked at from the side, the inside of the foot should not lie flat on the ground.

25

Making the breastplate

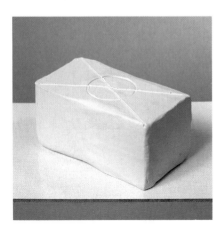

Draw the diagonals and the diameter of the head on a cube.

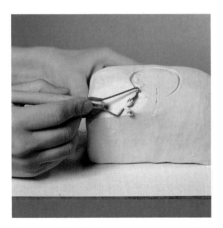

Use a modelling hook to slope the cube at the front and sideways.

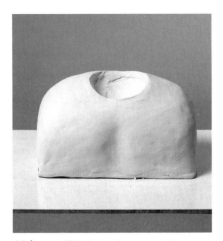

Make a small hollow in the centre of the front.

Prepare either a plasticine or modelling clay cube, which should be about 14cm (5½ in) long, 7cm (2¾ in) wide and 7cm (2¾ in) high. Use a ruler to draw two diagonals on the upper side of the cube, then draw a circle where they cross, which roughly corresponds to the circumference of the neck. To the left and right of this circle, scrape away some of the clay with a pot loop to shape the shoulders and the thorax, then smooth these over. Now make a small hollow in the middle of the front of the chest and also at the back. Round off the shoulder outwards and downwards. Use the pot loop to slightly hollow out the circle you have drawn, into which the neck will be inserted.

Casting and firing porcelain

To make the mould for the breastplate, place the model on a plastic plate or on a large board with the mould tin round it, see page 29. The distance of the model from the edge of the tin should be about 5cm (2in). Using a thick brush, dust the plate and the model with talcum powder as a means of separating them. In casting you must ensure that the layer of plaster sticks out about 5cm (2in) from the model. When the plaster is hard, the mould tin and the plaster are separated.

The hollow in the plaster is the mould into which the porcelain will be poured later. While it is still a leathery consistency, the breastplate cast is cut left and right. When the porcelain is finally dry, the breastplate is wiped with a sponge. Use a scalpel to cut the holes for the elastic support and the hole for the neck. Now the breastplate is ready for firing.

Baking modelling clay

After making the model from clay it is baked at 100°C (212°F) three times in the oven for about twenty minutes each time. The model is then covered

Use the modelling loop to make a hollow for the neck.

On the back of the cube draw a line to indicate the spine.

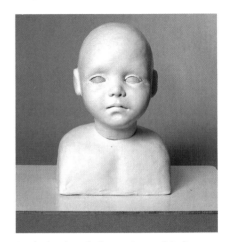

Set the head on the breastplate and fit them together.

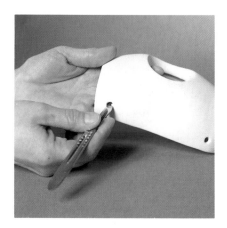

Use a scalpel to cut the holes for the elastic.

with aluminium foil which acts as a separator. Use a rolling-pin to roll out a modelling clay slab about 5mm (¼ in) thick, which should be as large as the upper surface of the model, and this is then laid over it. Into this slab, use the neck to press out the corresponding neck-rounding in the breastplate. As with the porcelain breastplate, the sides are cut on the left and right. Holes are pierced in the front and back of the model and a hole is made in the neck indentation. Bake the clay plate *lying on the model* for 20 minutes at 100°C (212°F). If necessary repeat the process. Before you take it off, the plate must be completely cold.

Elastic support

The porcelain head is attached to stretched elastic by means of a hook. For this you need strong 5mm (¼ in) elastic, a wooden ball about 1.5 to 2cm (⅝ to ¾ in) in diameter, with a hole bored through it, and strong 2mm (¹⁄₁₆ in) steel wire.

The wire is passed through the ball and bent into a hook, then pushed through the lower neck opening and hooked on to the ready-prepared breastplate. The elastic should be tightly stretched and firmly knotted, so that the head does not wobble.

Screw fixture

To secure the clay head you need a long screw, a felt or rubber washer, a metal spring and a nut, as well as some silicone lubricant. The screw is screwed head downwards into the neck with silicone, then continued through the hole in the neck indentation in the breastplate. From beneath the breastplate, the felt washer is put over the screw to protect the clay, then the spring and finally the nut. Make the spring as tight as possible. The head should turn but not wobble.

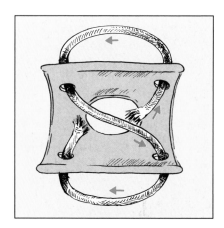

Thread the elastic through the breastplate and knot it.

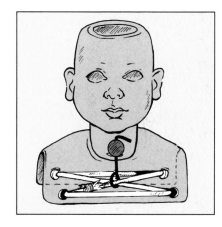

The porcelain head is held in the centre of the stretched elastic by a wire hook.

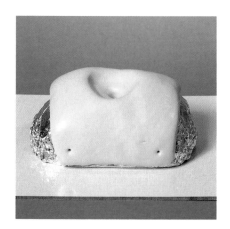

Lay a plate of modelling clay on the finished model and shape the breastplate.

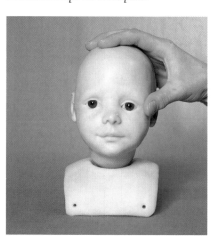

Set the finished head on the breastplate and mount it.

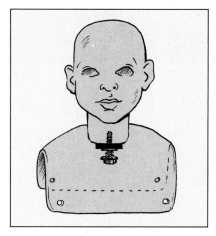

To hold the modelling clay head, a screw must be set into the head.

Making the mould for porcelain

Making the mould requires not only a certain amount of dexterity, but a precise method of working and an exact knowledge of the properties of the plaster material.

Plaster as a material

There are different types of plaster for different uses but it is best to use alabaster modelling or moulding plaster. The plaster must be stored in a dry place because it draws moisture from the air, which makes it stick together and become hard.

Plaster is mixed with water and, as a rule of thumb, use one part water, to two parts plaster. Use cold water because warm water speeds up the setting process. When mixing the plaster only use clean containers and tools, which are free from any plaster remains. Note especially that the plaster is always mixed into the water and the water is never poured into the plaster. Use a sieve to pour in the correct amount of plaster, then leave the plaster to soak for a minute.

Use a whisk or a beater to mix the plaster thoroughly, noting that the consistency must be sticky. Do not beat the mixture too hard, because this will create undesirable air bubbles. If it becomes too thick when you are mixing it, you should throw it away and begin again. If streaks form while you are mixing, you have either used plaster that is too fresh, or dirty water.

It is best to use a plastic or rubber bowl in which to mix the plaster. Be sure not to pour any surplus plaster down the drain as it will stick to the drain and cause a blockage. Let the remains of any plaster go dry in the bowl, and with a light pressure on the side of the bowl you can easily pull it away. All utensils should be cleaned immediately after use.

Overlap

Before you begin to make the mould, read this section carefully because you must know exactly what an overlap is and what effect it can have. To get some idea, let us look forward a couple of steps to the moment when the mould has to be opened. With a faultless and correctly prepared mould you remove the upper half vertically, but when individual parts, such as cheeks or forehead, overlap the cutting line, the model sticks to the mould. Parts jut out which get in the way when you want to remove the mould.

To make sure this does not happen, place your model horizontally in front of you and make absolutely sure that all the upward lines become narrower. The line from the chin to the neck is also important, and when you support the head for the mould, make sure that this line is vertical, and not going inwards.

In a two-part mould, modelled ears can also cause overlaps, so only make the ears on the porcelain blank. You must also remember that nowhere on the back of the head should be wider than the cutting line.

Material

Formica plate
Fine-grained clay
Metal set square
Mould tin
Strong adhesive tape
Eyeballs to bore knobs
Brush
Separating material

Mould tins should be open on at least one side, so that they can be easily

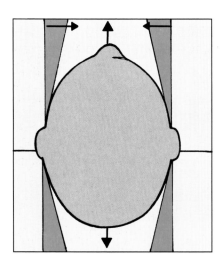

A mould without overlaps, which allows the upper and lower part to be removed without any problem.

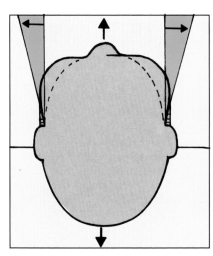

The upper part of the mould cannot be removed. It is stuck by the overlap between the cheek and the ear.

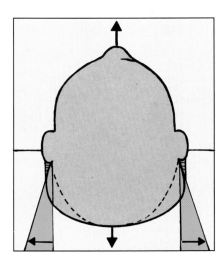

The lower part of the mould cannot be removed. It is stuck by the overlap between the ear and the back of the head.

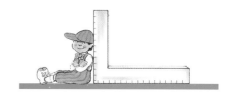

Support the head on a clay base. It must go over the edge of the base.

Use a set square to determine the contact points and mark them.

Clearly draw the cutting lines round the whole head.

detached from the mould. It is best to have metal strips made of tin, or copper sheeting, cut for you by a plumber and bent to form two equal right angles. A separating material is used to prevent the two halves of the plaster mould sticking together, so that it can be detached from the model when it is removed from the plaster cast. You can use a dusting of talcum powder, or a light application of floor polish as a separating medium.

Making a mould in two parts

On the formica board make a thin clay base and lay the head to be moulded on this base. The head must be supported by the clay base in such a way that the line between the chin and neck does not run inwards, otherwise you will get an overlap. As the mould consists of two joining upper and lower parts, you must first find the cutting line, and in order to mark it, place a set square upright round the head. Mark all the places where the set square touches the head, then use a sharp object to draw a clear line on the head. This joining line is the cutting line between the two halves of the mould.

The head is now embedded in the clay exactly at the height of the cutting line. Do this *very* carefully. You must not allow it to drop under the line, or bring the clay up higher than the line, as you may create overlaps.

Embed the head up to the cutting line into the clay.

Position the moulding tin. Hold it together on the outside and support it with clay.

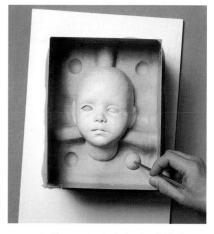

Use eyeballs to make the holes for the locks.

Making the mould for porcelain

Pour the plaster over your cupped hand, to eliminate air bubbles.

Clay bed

The clay bed should surround the head for at least 6cm (2¼ in). This is so that the tin can be pressed well into the clay and the plaster cast is not too thin. Place the halves of the tin round the clay, and stick them together with a wide firm rubber band or packing tape. Support the mould tin thus created on the outside with clay. If the container is not accurately joined, the plaster may leak out. On the inside of the tin, smear clear petroleum jelly on to the joins of the two halves, see page 29.

Handles

To make handles, form thin rolls of clay and lay them on the inner wall of the tin. Press them with your finger on to the mould tin and the clay.

Pouring hole

When preparing the mould you must make provision for a pouring hole. Make a 3 to 4cm (1¼ to 1½ in) roll of clay and cut it through lengthwise. Lay one half with the flat cut side downwards on the clay bed between the head and the wall of the mould.

Knob locks

In order to ensure that the two halves of the mould do not slip out of alignment, when you pour in the porcelain plaster, use a locking system to secure them. To do this, use eyeballs to make a hollow in at least three corners of the clay bed. This hollow shows on the reverse side as a knob, so it is called a 'knob' lock.

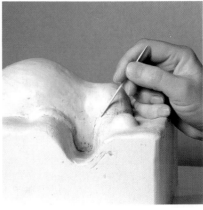

Carefully clean off any clay remnants from the cutting line.

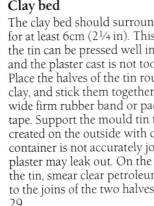

Set the handles and the pouring supports.

When the plaster is completely hard, take away the tin.

Now remove the clay completely from one side of the mould.

This is how the finished mould looks with knob locks.

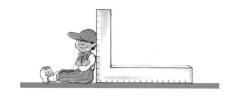

Separator

The mould is now ready for casting, except for one thing – the separator. Use a soft brush to spread either talcum powder or floor polish over the whole of the upper surface. The separating agent should be spread thinly, but evenly. Only now can you touch the plaster.

Pouring the plaster

If at all possible, have someone to assist you when you are pouring the plaster. If the plaster is poured over an outstretched cupped hand, it gets rid of any air bubbles which may have appeared during the mixing. The plaster should be poured slowly into the mould in one go.

Before you can continue working, the plaster must set. During the setting process it becomes warm and only when this warmth has cooled off can the mould tin be removed.

The clay is now separated from the plaster. Clean the remains of clay and separating material off the cutting line, so that you do not get thick seams later. Now set the mould tins round the plaster half, and stick them carefully together again. As before, smear the joins and set in the handles and pouring supports. Spread separating agent on the plaster and the model, as set plaster can also bind with fresh plaster. Without separating the two parts, the mould would weld together.

When the second casting is cold, you can take away the tin and separate the two halves. Let them dry in the mould and clean them with a stiff brush. You can remove any plasticine remnants with a cloth soaked in acetone.

Arms and legs

If you have followed the instructions for making the two-part mould for the head, it should not be a problem to make the moulds for the arms and the legs, using the same principle. As given for the head, the arms and legs are supported on a clay base and the cutting line is drawn in.

The foot is set with the heel upwards. The separation line runs from the ankle sideways to the top of the foot, along the middle of the calf. When the heel and ankle are strongly modelled you must ensure that no overlaps occur.

Put in the hand, palm upwards. Be especially careful that the separation line between thumb and index finger is correctly drawn in. It requires patience to mark the separation lines cleanly between the fingers. If you are not careful at this stage, you may tear off the finger when you open the mould. Finger and toe-nails are added as fine details to the plaster blank at a later stage.

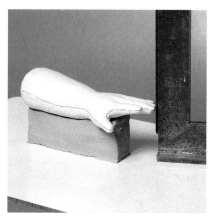

Draw the cutting line for arm and hand.

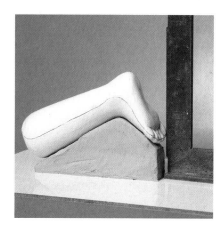

Draw the cutting line for leg and foot, as for the arm and hand.

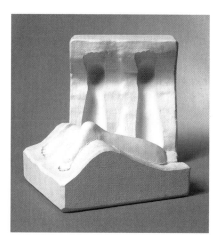

This is how the mould for the foot and leg looks when it is finished.

Porcelain

Porcelain dough can be bought ready prepared in airtight plastic containers. Long storage may make parts of it stick to the bottom and sides of the container and in order to obtain an even consistency, the porcelain must be stirred before use. Small particles which do not dissolve when stirred can be filtered out with a special sieve, or a piece of nylon netting. As stirring may introduce air bubbles into the porcelain, you should let it stand for a little while before you cast it. When casting, pour the porcelain into a measuring jug with a spout, which will enable you to fill the mould in a thin stream up to the top.

Porcelain casting

Before use, the moulds must be carefully cleaned with a soft brush. Dry moulds must also be sprinkled inside with a little distilled water and a new mould should be given at least two sprinklings. The mould, firmly held together by rubber bands, is filled up to the pouring hole with porcelain. The plaster mould immediately draws water out of the dough, so that the porcelain sinks. After a few minutes, pour in a little more porcelain, until the original level is reached again.

Repeat this process once or twice and when you have made a layer 4 to 6cm (1½ to 2¼ in) thick on the upper edge, the surplus porcelain is poured back into the container. The room temperature, consistency of the porcelain and the dampness of the mould will determine how long you have to continue pouring. Large moulds obviously take longer than small ones and hand and foot moulds can sometimes be cast in a matter of 5 to 7 minutes.

Now leave the mould standing with the pouring hole downwards for at least one hour. Do not open the mould until the porcelain has become leathery. Lay the head mould face upwards and carefully take off the upper half, then take the cast porcelain out of the other half of the mould and use a flat knife to knock off the

pouring supports. This automatically creates the hole in the top of the head. If the moulded porcelain sinks in, then you have either opened the mould too soon or suction was created when you were pouring in the porcelain.

Lay all the moulded parts in a warm, airy place to dry. Place the head with the head hole downwards and only when the porcelain has become white, will it be dry enough to be worked on further.

Firing porcelain

Before the porcelain blank can be fired, add the fine details, see page 34. If you do not have your own oven you must find a suitable one you can use in your neighbourhood. Many craft shops offer the use of a firing oven, or perhaps there is another doll maker nearby, who will help you. Another alternative is to approach your adult education institute, who may be able to provide this facility. If you decide to buy an oven, the following advice will be helpful.

Your own oven

Before you buy, seek the advice of your dealer and explain the purpose for which you require the oven. Of course, it will also largely depend on how much money you want to spend.

Nowadays, technology is so advanced that you can also buy automatic ovens at a reasonable price. Before you make your choice, also make sure that you have a suitably wired socket.

It is not easy for anyone without experience of firing an oven to adjust the temperature controls and you must remember that the oven has to reach a firing temperature of 1,260°C (2,300°F). With cheap ovens, the firing temperature can often only be regulated imprecisely and the result is badly fired objects, which cannot be painted, or which are misshapen.

During the firing process, porcelain shrinks by approximately 20 per cent and as this change occurs in the oven, it should not be laid on a firm base but on a thin layer of clean sand. It is best to bake new sand in the oven for the first time without placing anything on it.

Porcelain consists of about 50 per cent kaolin and 25 per cent each of quartz and feldspar, and it is mixed with water. Every raw material in this mixture melts at a different temperature and for this reason you should never switch the oven to full heat straight away. Put it on for one to two hours at about 250°C (482°F) and leave the air hole open. Then set the oven at medium temperature for three to four hours, this time with the air hole closed. Only then should you let the oven operate at full blast. If the porcelain is not fired in stages, the material may lose its shape, and not be fired right through, or the upper surface of the porcelain may acquire ugly marks and blemishes.

Henrietta is in a dreamy mood! She is wearing a high-waisted salmon-pink dress with a double flounce at the hem.
A large lace collar covers her shoulders and the sleeves also have neat lace cuffs.

Fine details

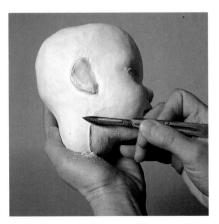

Carefully remove the seam with a scalpel.

The porcelain blank cannot be fired until you have added the final details. You will need a scourer with a rough and a smooth side, a pointed scalpel and a rounded scalpel, a thin knitting needle or toothpick to engrave lines, a scraper to make hollows, as well as wooden balls of different sizes, which are fixed to a handle.

To engrave fine details, use various sizes of cow hair brushes, a synthetic brush number 6 and a thick, soft goat hair brush for dusting. While you are working wear a mask because fine porcelain dust can be harmful to the lungs.

Head and neck hole

Begin by removing the casting seam using the pointed scalpel. Cut out the head hole and the neck hole neatly. Be particularly careful with the neck hole and use only a slight twisting movement of the scalpel to cut an opening about 1.5cm (¾ in) in diameter. Then rub all unevenness flat with the rough side of the scouring sponge and polish with the smooth side.

Now use the scalpel to cut out the eye-openings, but be extra careful with the upper eyelid. The eye socket is cut into the head so that the glass eyes can be inserted after firing. Use the round scalpel to scrape out enough porcelain to allow the eyeballs to fit in. Cover the wooden ball with a nylon stocking and use it to polish the opening carefully until the eye fits into the socket.

The nostrils are deepened with the scraper and finished off with the synthetic brush, as are the sides of the nose, the mouth and the chin.

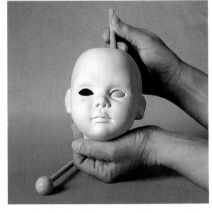

Use the wooden ball to smooth the eye sockets from the inside.

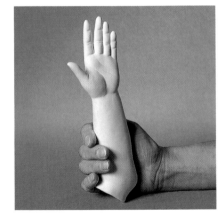

Use the scouring sponge, first on the rough side and then on the smooth side, to rub down the porcelain.

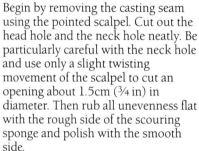

Draw the lines on the palm of the hand precisely and model them.

Cut a hole underneath the neck with the scalpel.

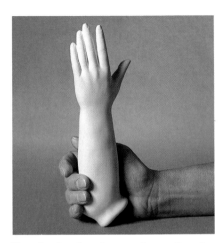

Use a brush to form finger and toe-nails and polish them.

Ears

Shaping the ears requires great care and at first glance, their many lines and contours are quite bewildering. The diagram shows you the various steps required to shape each ear, but do make sure that they match.

The first step is to draw the groove of the ear in the shape of an open figure nine and mark the point above the ear lobe. The next stage is to round off the ear lobe and in the upper half of the ear, gouge out a little triangular hollow. Check whether the scraping marks can still be seen and smooth over any unevenness with the cow hair brush, and then with the synthetic brush, as every rough place becomes a problem to paint after firing.

Arms and legs are worked in the same way as given for the head.

Fingers and toes

You should take great care with the palms of the hands and the finger and toe-nails, see opposite page. Engrave the lines on the palm and use a brush for the parts which have to be rounded. Toe and finger-nails are slightly curved. Draw the nails and then work on them with the brush.

Before firing, inspect all the parts critically once more in different lights. Look for scraping marks and any areas of unevenness in strong sunlight. Study the doll's expression and the play of light and shade at a window, preferably one with a north-facing light. Remove every speck of dust with the goat hair brush, or blow it off with a hair dryer. After firing you will no longer be able to make any corrections, and it would be a pity to miss anything at this crucial stage.

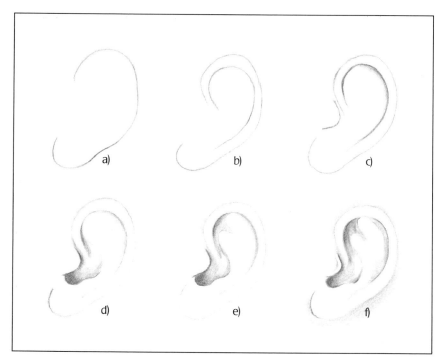

Step-by-step shaping of the ears: a) unformed; b) groove in the shape of a figure 9; c) corner; d) hollowing it out; e) triangle in the upper ear; f) the finished ear.

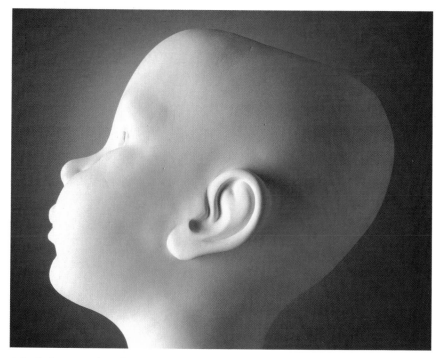

A finished ear. Note how the ear slopes towards the back of the head and its shape and inner structure.

Painting

Painting is one of the most pleasant and exciting aspects of doll making, because this is what makes the doll come alive. With a little patience and skill the features can be lightly sketched in, but if you are in too much of a hurry, all your efforts may be wasted. Here, as is so often the case, practice makes perfect, but it is also essential to spend some time deciding on the mood and expression you wish to capture.

There are special porcelain paints available for porcelain dolls, but, providing that you first apply a foundation, oil paints are recommended to paint dolls made from modelling clay. The following fundamental principles should be studied before beginning to paint the face.

Materials

For this stage you will need two fine brushes, size 0/0 to 3/0, to paint the eyebrows and eyelashes, and a flat-ended brush, called a 'cat's tongue' brush, for the lips. You also need a glazed white tile, or a china saucer for mixing the paints. Be careful not to let any loose brush hairs get caught in the paint.

Type of doll and expression

Consider what hair and eye colour your doll should have, as this determines the colour choice for eyebrows and lashes and the basic skin tint. Blonde or auburn-haired people have a paler skin tone than brunette or dark-haired people. Children do not wear lipstick, so be careful with the use of strong reds. In order to obtain the most natural shades, you need to mix many colours. For fantasy dolls, however, let your imagination run wild and combine as many colours as you wish.

Eyebrows and lashes have their own special function. The eyebrows are not set on the forehead but on the brow, and their hairs grow horizontally to protect the eyes from foreign bodies, such as dust and drops of sweat. The eyebrows should not be set too close together as this will give a grim expression. The lower eyelashes should also be painted naturally and should not be too long.

The pupil is responsible for regulating the light falling into the eye and in a strong light it grows smaller, while in a dim light it grows larger. Our eyes, however, are not just for seeing but are also the mirror of our moods and emotions. The pupils also grow smaller when we feel anger or dislike and larger when we feel sympathy or attraction. Take this into consideration and do not paint the pupils too small. Also look out for this characteristic when you buy glass eyes.

Full lips are more appealing than thin ones, so make the upper lip full when you paint it. The lower lip runs into the upper lip, so it should not be drawn right to the corner of the mouth.

Painting modelling clay dolls

Before beginning the actual painting with oils, a foundation must be laid for the features and water-based or acrylic model paints are suitable for this.

The oil paint colours you need are white, black, burnt sienna, red, chrome yellow, and Prussian blue. Green is not necessary because you can mix a bright green from Prussian blue and chrome yellow. Buy small tubes because you only need a small amount.

Before you begin work you must thin the oil paints with paint thinner, turpentine, or a turpentine substitute. To clean your brushes use nitrate solution.

Natural looking shades are obtained by mixing colours. Here are a few tips about what to use for different dolls' eyes, eyelashes, eyebrows and lips.

Eyes			Eyebrows		
Blue eyes:	→	Mid-blue (Prussian blue), white and black.	Blonde hair:	→	Ochre or light brown with yellow and a touch of red.
Green eyes:	→	Green, brown and white.	Red hair:	→	Light brown and a little red.
Brown eyes:	→	Mid-brown, dark brown and burnt sienna for shading.	Brown hair:	→	Light brown and dark brown.
			Dark hair:	→	Dark brown or dark brown and black.
Eyelashes		Light brown to dark brown with some black. Never use just black as this looks too hard.	**Mouth**		Light red, light brown and a little white for highlighting.

Eye and parts of the eye

As the modelling clay is already coloured, a basic tint is unnecessary and you can begin painting the foundation for the eyes straight away. Cover the whole eye with a white glaze base. Allow the paint to dry for about two hours, then you can paint the iris with the colour you have chosen. After another two hours drying time, the pupils come next. Only when the foundation is completely dry, after a period of about 24 hours, can you go on to use oil paint.

For this stage, spread out a newspaper over your work surface and have ready a flat saucer containing paint thinner, and another with nitrate solution. Press out a pea-sized drop of oil paint on to the tile and use the brush to put a drop of paint thinner at the edge of the paint. Using the point of the brush, mix enough paint with it to make an almost fluid liquid. The colour is easy to spread when it has the consistency of condensed milk. Use the point of the brush only to take up some of the paint and begin to paint.

Always work from the top downwards so as not to spoil parts you have finished, and begin with the eyebrows, then the eyes, the lashes on the lower eyelid and finally the mouth. Every time you change colour, wash the brush carefully. Dip it into the nitrate solution and softly draw it over the newspaper, as this makes the hairs of the brush go back to a clean point.

Eye foundation

Apply the eye colours in the following order: all the area white, then the iris in the desired colour, finally the pupil.

Eyebrows

Draw the eyebrows and set the basic line, then fill in this line above and below with small strokes.

Oil painting the eyes

Add colours in the same order as for the eye foundation. Shade the iris very softly, perhaps using grey shading for the rim of the iris, with white highlights if desired.

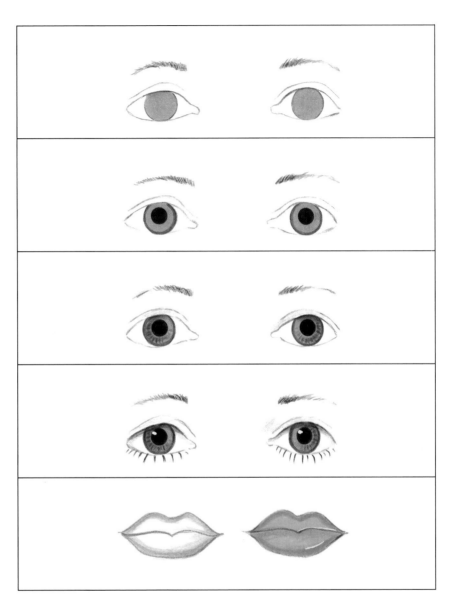

Eyelashes

Only paint in the lower eyelashes, as the upper eyelashes made of hair will be stuck on.

Lips and parts of the mouth

Paint the contours of the mouth and then spread the colour inwards. Use the cat's tongue brush to apply the lip colour and blot it with a paper tissue.

A child's mouth should be delicately coloured and transparent.

Although modelling clay absorbs colour quickly, oil paints take several days to dry. Only when you are sure that the paint will not smudge, can you dab a little brown-toned lip colour on to a paper tissue and use your finger to rub in a little on the tip of the nose, the chin and the cheeks.

Painting

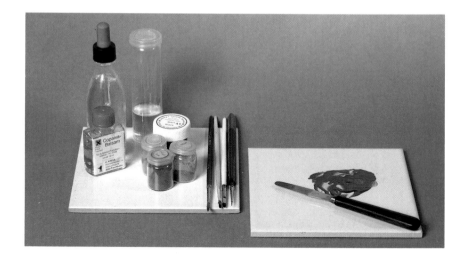

Palm balsam or oil, lavender oil and oil of cloves, powder paints in the desired colours, cat's tongue brush, brushes in various sizes, tile on which to mix the paints, spatula.

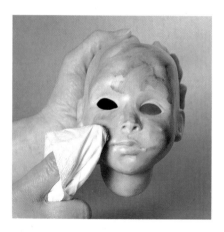

Spread foundation evenly on the previously oiled head.

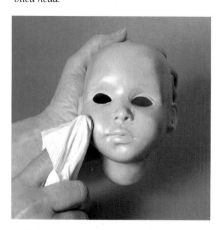

Rub the foundation in, leaving no smears.

Painting porcelain dolls

Porcelain colours usually come as powder in small packets or bottles, but sometimes they can be obtained as a paste. They are available from craft shops.

To make the colour adhere to the surface of the porcelain, you need a paint 'medium'. You can use a palm balsam or oil, clove or lavender oil, or a suitable thick oil for this purpose. Some firms even offer the appropriate paint medium for particular colours. Seek the advice of your stockist before you buy your requirements.

Paints from different suppliers may also require different firing temperatures. If you have no previous experience in using porcelain paints, do not mix products from different manufacturers.

To clean your brush it is best to use pure turpentine, or white spirit. Good brushes are expensive, and it pays to protect them. Store them in a jar with their tips upwards, or put them in a tin box with a turpentine-soaked rag as this keeps them soft.

The colours are mixed on a tile or glass dish with a small pliable spatula. Place some powder on the tip of the spatula, put it on the tile and drip the medium on to it, drop by drop, through an eye-dropper. To test the consistency, draw a line through the paint mixture with the edge of the spatula. When the paint runs back together again, it is ready to use.

Even when you have used tinted porcelain, the head, breastplate, arms and legs must be given a foundation. Because the porcelain parts may feel a little rough after baking, you must first prepare them for the foundation, as the surface should be silky-smooth. Polish the porcelain with a sponge until it is ready, then wash it with water, or white spirit. Hold the head firmly by the head hole so that you have no problem spreading the foundation all over it, then rub the head over with oil. Make sure the oil is evenly applied then wipe off any surplus with a paper handkerchief. Put this tissue out of reach immediately so that you do not use it by mistake when spreading the foundation.

For the foundation you can mix brown and red shades. Apply the colour on the face, neck and sides of the head, then use a clean cloth to spread the colour evenly and wipe off the surplus. Don't panic if the foundation process is not successful in one go, as you can always wash it off with lukewarm soapy water.

If you are a beginner, be sparing with the foundation and repeat the process after firing if the colour looks too pale. Remember the corner of the

A delicately painted porcelain doll. The colours you use for skin, eyelashes, eyebrows, and lips, are a matter of choice.

mouth, the eye socket and the ears must also be covered with foundation. Colour the breastplate, arms and legs in the same way. Put all the porcelain pieces in the oven for the first firing, taking care that it is at the correct temperature.

The actual painting of the porcelain should be undertaken in the following order: the eyebrows, lashes, nostrils and, finally, the lips. Always begin painting on the left-hand side of the face, otherwise you run the risk of smudging finished parts with your hand. For drawing you can use a pencil, but it is best to paint freehand without drawing beforehand. Any brush stroke which is not correct can easily be erased with a cotton bud and white spirit and practice eventually makes perfect, as you can only learn to paint by painting. Painting the lower eyelashes, however, is a little more difficult, as you must apply each stroke separately with a steady hand. You can correct individual lashes with the tip of a toothpick, but as you may smudge them, it is often better to begin all over again.

The colour must be spread very evenly on the mouth. Draw the contours with the cat's tongue brush and stroke the colour inwards. Then wipe off any surplus paint with a paper handkerchief and even it up again. It is up to you how vividly you paint the lips – but soft shades appear more natural. With the remains of the paint used for the lips, you can paint the finger and toe-nails. Everything is now ready for the second firing.

After firing, the rouge is applied and you should choose a warm red shade. Follow the same order as given for the foundation, noting that the forehead, nose, cheeks and chin are first oiled and then rouged. Rub the rouge on to the forehead, nose and chin a little more firmly than the cheeks, as a rosy glow on these areas makes the face look more lifelike. You can also put a little rouge on the backs of the hands, the outside of the arms and the shin bone. When you have made your last brush stroke you are ready for the third firing.

Cloth body

For a doll's body of 48 to 64cm (19 to 25¼ in), you will need 40cm (16in) of unbleached hard-wearing cotton material and about 1.5m (1⅝ yds) cotton cord.

The body consists of four basic parts, see patterns on pages 42–5; 1. Back. 2. Back leg. 3. Front and front leg. 4. Arm.

You will also need to cut some bias strips about 2.5cm (1in) wide for the neck, arm and leg bindings. For this you require a strip of cotton material 20cm (7¾ in) long for the neck finishing, two 12cm (4¾ in) long strips for the arms and two 16cm (6¼ in) strips for the legs.

Cutting out and sewing

For cutting out, fold the material double, noting that 1cm (½ in) seam allowance is included in the pattern. Pin your pattern pieces on to the fabric and then cut them out. Before removing the pattern pieces, mark the darts either using tailor's tacks or a carbon pencil. Join all the darts first, two on the back piece and one on the armhole. Next, sew the top of the back leg piece to the bottom edge of the back piece, taking care to match the side seams. Join the front piece to the back piece along the side seam leaving 3cm (1¼ in) of the seam open at the top for the arms.

Now pin the edge of your bias binding strips to the edge of the arms and legs, right sides together. Stitch a seam 5mm (¼ in) from the edge. Turn under and press the binding's raw edge to the same amount. Turn the binding to the wrong side of the garment and slip-stitch close to the stitched line. Machine round the hem again to fix the binding firmly.

Next, join the shoulder seams, centre front and centre back seams, taking care to leave an opening in the back seam as indicated on the pattern. Finally stitch the inside leg seam, leaving the binding open. Bind the neck edge in the same way as you have done for the arms and legs.

Join the arm seams, leaving the

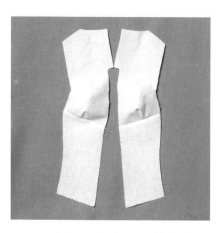

First join the leg and back parts of the body.

Join the side of the back to the front.

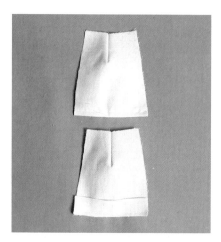

Do not forget to carefully neaten the arm and leg bindings.

Join the back seam, the shoulder seam and the centre front seam.

Sew the inside leg seam.

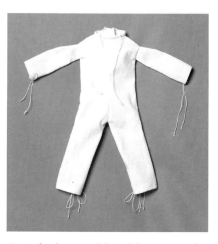

Set in the sleeves and thread the cotton cord through the channels.

binding open, and then stitch them to the body, noting that the dart in each ~rm runs parallel with the shoulder ~m. Thread lengths of cotton cord rough the bindings at the arms, legs .d neck. These will be used later to)ld the stuffing and wire in place, and , secure the ceramic limbs and head ι position.

Wire frame

To turn the empty cotton shape into a body you need a wire frame and padding material. The frame is made from wire and plastic bobbins, and this supports the body and holds it in the right position. Cut two equal pieces of wire, each 60cm (23½ in) long. Now thread one wire from the left and the other from the right through the bobbin. Bend about 21cm (8¼ in) of wire downwards for the legs and the rest upwards. The upper wires are twisted together and held vertically by another bobbin. When you have threaded the wires through the bobbin bend them sideways, one to the left and the other to the right.

Filling

For filling the body you can use wadding made of either synthetic fibre or wool. A third possibility is synthetic granules. After you have made the wire frame, fit it into the body and begin padding evenly round the wire. Pad the body tightly because it has to support the weight of the head and the breastplate without sinking inwards. Arms and legs are stuffed more loosely, otherwise they stick out too much from the body. Wind foam round the wire ends so that they do not damage the porcelain, and slightly tighten the cords.

Stuff the body evenly right up to the seams.

This is how the padded body should look when it is ready.

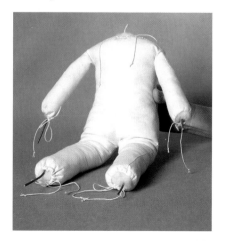

Stick foam over the ends of the wire which are still protruding.

Fit the wire frame into the body.

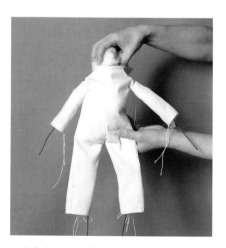

Pad the body on all sides round the wire.

Pattern pieces for the doll's body

These pattern pieces are intended for reuse, so do not remove them from the book. They have been reproduced to the same size needed to fit the instructions given for the clay and porcelain models in the Workshop section. You can easily reduce or enlarge them to any size you require, by photocopying them on a machine which provides these facilities. As an alternative, you can make your own graph.

For both methods you must first make a copy, using tracing or grease-proof paper. Draw round each section and mark each piece clearly with the printed instructions. To make either a reduced or an enlarged copy, divide each tracing into evenly-sized squares, about 2cm (¾ in) apart. Then cut a piece of drawing paper for each section, which will allow for the sizes required. Divide these pieces of paper in the same way as the tracings, with the same number of horizontal and vertical squares.

Now look at each square of the tracings in turn, beginning at the top left-hand corner. Ignore all the empty squares but as soon as you come to a square which contains any markings, find the equivalent square on the drawing paper and transfer all these lines. Make sure you reproduce each line in the same position and to the correct proportions of the drawing paper. When you have completed each section, it may be necessary to even out any small irregularities along the dividing lines of each square.

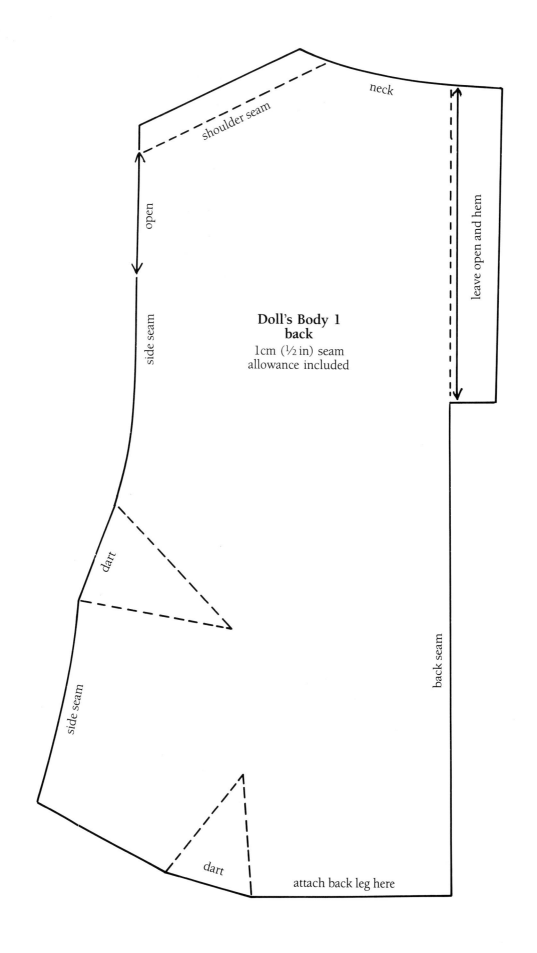

shoulder seam

neck

open

leave open and hem

side seam

**Doll's Body 1
back**

1cm (½ in) seam
allowance included

dart

back seam

side seam

dart

attach back leg here

43

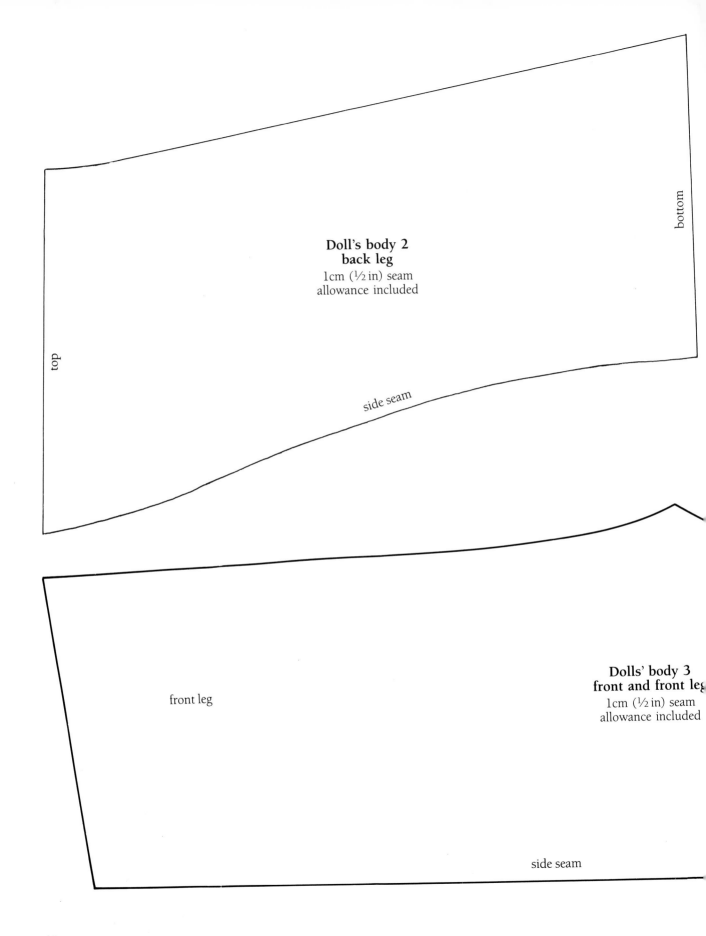

**Doll's body 2
back leg**

1cm (½ in) seam
allowance included

bottom

top

side seam

front leg

**Dolls' body 3
front and front leg**

1cm (½ in) seam
allowance included

side seam

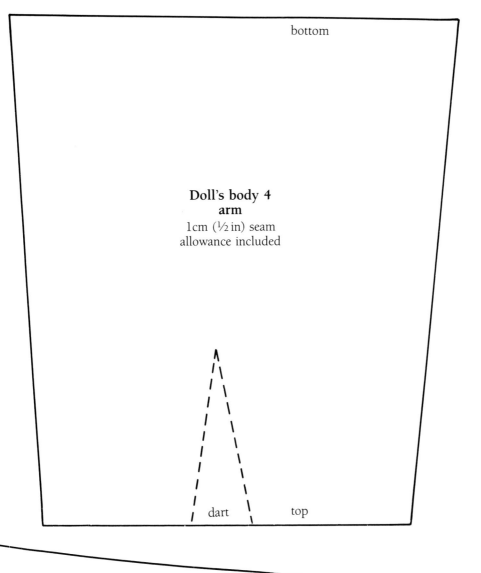

bottom

Doll's body 4
arm
1cm (½ in) seam
allowance included

dart   top

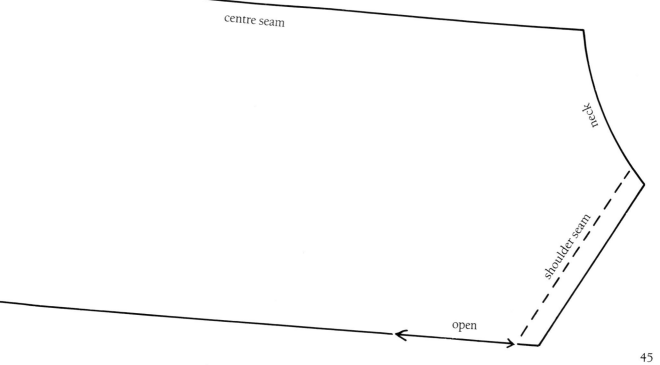

centre seam

neck

shoulder seam

open

Assembling the doll

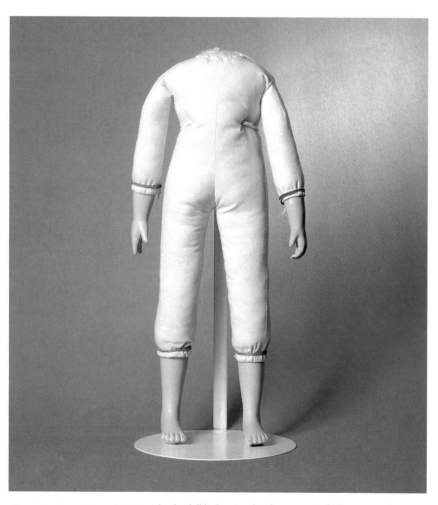

Correct posture is important to make the doll look natural. When you attach the arms make sure that the palm of each hand is facing inwards.

Body language

We express our feelings not only by language and facial expression but also through our gestures and posture. For example, a sad or depressed person may have drooping shoulders, a child who is embarrassed may stare at the ground and stand with toes pointing inwards, or if we are threatened, we may protect our head with our arm.

Through our posture and gestures we unconsciously express vitality, aggression, passivity, discomfort and many other emotions. If you observe people carefully, you will see that their facial expression ties in with their bodily behaviour.

Body posture

The posture of the body is important when assembling your doll. You should note that when standing at ease, the arms hang down with the palms facing inwards. The feet, and therefore the legs, must be attached so that the toes point outwards. Arms and legs are set in this position, and from this neutral stance, you can make your doll stand, sit or lie as you want.

Insert the arms and legs into the cloth body and draw the cotton cords at the arm and leg ends together and knot them firmly, then cut off the spare cord and tuck the knots inside the cloth. When the limbs are glued on, fasten with rubber bands and keep them in position until the glue is completely dry, then you can remove the rubber bands.

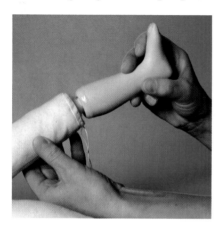

Stick the arms and legs on with glue.

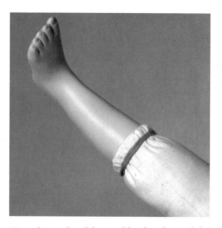

Knot the cord and fix a rubber band round the sticking place.

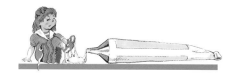

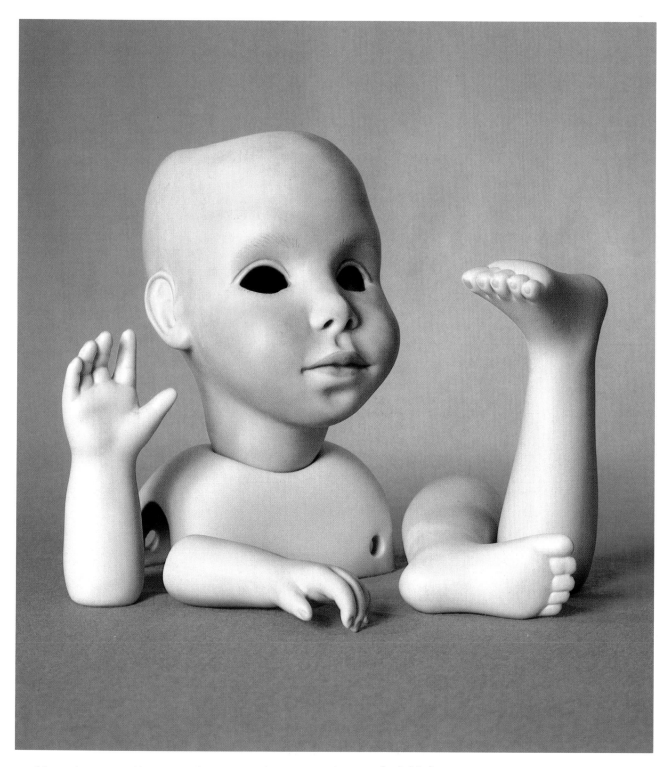

Head, breastplate, arms and legs are complete, so you can begin to mount them on to the cloth body.

Eyes and wigs

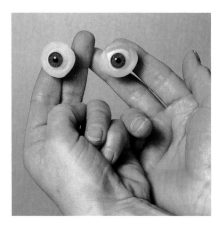

Place a thin roll of eye wax round the eyes.

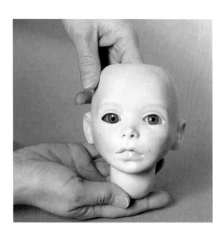

Fit the eyes into the head and adjust them to the required position.

Use the back of a small spoon to plaster the eyes into the head.

The expression in glass eyes, also the choice of hair-style will add the final finishing touches to your doll. You will need the following items:—

Eyes
Wax for setting in the eyes
Small bowl of water and plaster
Small spoon
Toothpick
Scissors
Rubber solution
Head crown (purchased with wig)
Glue
Rubber bands
Eyelashes and wig

Eyes

There is a wide choice of eyes and wigs available and their colour should match the doll's complexion, see pages 36–7. Among others there are oval and round hemispherical eyes, hollow and filled round glass eyes, glass eyes with the iris painted in and hand-blown crystal eyes. It is best to choose round eyes that correspond to the eye's natural shape. The eye dimension is given in millimetres (fractions of an inch) and depends on the size of the eye socket. Measure the distance from one corner of the eye to the other and add about 3mm ($\frac{1}{8}$ in). The iris must touch the upper and lower lid.

Before you set in the eyes you should remember that the direction of the gaze also has an effect on the doll's facial expression. If you set the eyes looking outwards the doll may look dreamy, slightly dazed or even sad. If the eyes are looking down the expression is embarrassed, ashamed or even upset. You can make your doll look straight at you, but in this case it should be looking slightly up, because children are smaller than adults and naturally look up at them.

Begin by putting a ring of slightly kneaded eye wax round each eye, then take an eye between two fingers and push it into the eye socket. Turn the eye until it is looking in the right direction and then press it firmly in

Leave the plaster to dry, laying the head face downwards.

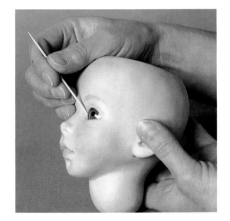

Remove any surplus wax and plaster with a toothpick.

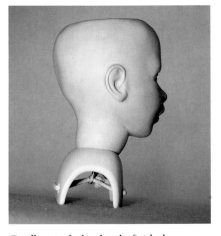

Finally, join the head to the finished breastplate.

Stick the head crown over the hole in the head and hold it with a rubber band.

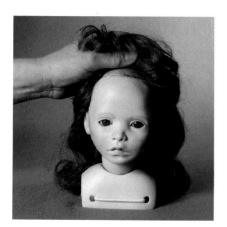

Stick the wig of your choice over the head crown when it is dry.

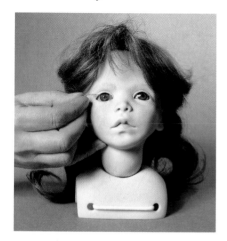

Carefully glue on the eyelashes and adjust their position.

with wax. To make sure that the doll is not squinting, turn the head sideways. From this angle it is easiest to see whether both pupils are at the same level and pointing in the same direction. Now stir the plaster, making sure it is not too liquid, and plaster the eyes inside the head, using a small spoon, then lay the head to dry face downwards. When the plaster is dry you can remove any surplus wax or plaster with a toothpick.

Wigs

Artificial and real hair wigs, also mohair wigs can be obtained in a wide variety of prices today. These also come complete with a head crown for closing the hole in the top of the head, but you can make your own from hessian. It is important that the wig does not overwhelm the doll, that is, the hair-style should be appropriate and not too startling. To measure the circumference of the head, put the tape measure over the ears and take it round the forehead and the back of the head.

As we have already described in the chapter on making the breastplate, see page 26, before attaching the wig the head is joined to the breastplate. If the head crown does not fit exactly you can cut it to the correct size with scissors and then stick it firmly over the head hole. To keep it in place while the glue is drying, put a rubber band round the head and under the chin.

When you attach the wig, hold the hair back with one hand and use your other hand to draw the wig over the head, over which you have already spread the glue. Measure the length of the lashes on the upper eyelid and cut them to the required length. Put a little glue on the edge of the eyelid and press the lashes quickly on to the upper eyelid. You can use a needle to adjust the lashes a little.

Finally, you have only to attach the head firmly to the body and, at last, you can enjoy your finished doll.

Mount the head and breastplate on to, or into, the body.

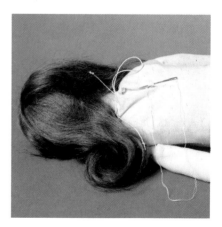

Carefully close the back seam of the body with small stitches.

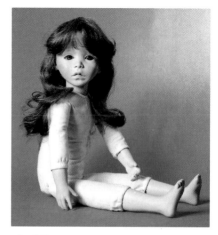

The doll is now ready and waiting for its clothing.

Clothing for dolls

Clothes maketh the person and also the doll! Any doll can be given a completely different personality by the clothes especially made for it. They provide the dot on the letter 'i', so we should give them careful consideration.

The delicate face of a doll is emphasized by clothes made from fine fabrics and embellished with lace. A cheeky urchin, on the other hand, looks better in jeans and a stripy jumper. A neat little schoolboy would be at home in a nostalgic sailor suit, or a demure little girl in a cotton dress with white collar and a dainty pinafore. But contrasts can also look original, and in real life we do not find any children dressed permanently in their Sunday best.

Choosing the clothes

The doll's wardrobe must, of course, consist of clothes that can be donned and removed, even if the dolls are not intended as playthings. It is also recommended that the fabrics should be washable, or can be cleaned, so it is a good idea to finish off the inner seams neatly. It would be a pity if after all your hard work they came undone in the wash.

Dolls' clothes only look attractive when they fit well, so take care not to cut them too skimpily. Tack the clothes carefully together first, then try them on the doll before you machine them. In a woman's dress it does not matter if the seam is 5mm (¼ in) out but this slight difference can determine whether the dress fits a doll properly. A dress made to a simple pattern can be decorated with lace, frills, ribbons, bows and flounces, but be careful not to overdo it. Gather or pleat skirts neatly, so that they fall properly.

Dress

A dress looks particularly childlike when the bodice is cut short. This dress fastens at the back and has a neckband, or collar. You must cut the left and the right sleeve to fit opposite sides and the same applies to the

sections of the collar. Sew the shoulder and side seams of the bodice and then the opening at the back.

Gather the sleeves at the shoulder and wrist, then join the sleeve seams and set the sleeves into the bodice. Sew the skirt seam, leaving 3cm (1¼ in) open at the top, and gather or pleat the skirt right along the lower edge of the bodice. When you attach the skirt to the bodice, make sure that the skirt seam comes in the centre of the bodice back. Neaten and finish off the opening with press studs and complete the sleeves with neat cuffs.

Prepare the collar and sew each half to the appropriate side of the neck. The top of the collar goes over the neck and is attached with small stitches to the inside of the dress. Lastly hem the lower edge of the skirt.

Petticoat

For the petticoat, cut a strip of material 24 × 80cm (9½ × 31½ in) and attach 1.5cm (⅝ in) gathered lace or broderie anglaise along one long edge, then sew up the seam leaving 4cm (1½ in) open at the top. Now gather the upper edge to fit the waist size of the doll and sew on the waistband. This is fastened with a button and loop.

Vest

The vest is the same for boys and girls. First join the back parts at the open edge, as shown on the pattern, and then sew the shoulder seams. Neaten the armholes and machine the outer seams, then sew round the bottom of the vest. Lastly, sew bias binding to the neck edge, which you can also make into a small stand-up collar. The vest is fastened at the back with press studs.

Trousers and jacket

Both trouser legs are cut as one piece. The boy's trousers reach to the ankle, the girl's long panties to the knee. Measure the length of the inner and outer leg accordingly.

The trousers are cut out in two pieces. First join the two legs on the inside then sew the back and front seams. For the boy's trousers, put in

the four darts indicated. For the girl's long panties, use pleats instead. Now sew on the trouser band. In order to adjust it round the waist you can thread elastic or, in the girl's case a satin ribbon, through the trouser band. The boy's trousers are hemmed at the bottom but you can gather the girl's panties with elastic and finish them off with lace.

The sailor jacket, on page 62, is open at the front but is held together by the tie at the neck and a draw-string threaded through the hem. First join the shoulder and side seams and set in the sleeves. Then sew the collar to the neck and neaten the front edges. Hem the jacket at the bottom and thread a cord, or elastic, through the hem to give a blouson effect. The sleeves are finished off with cuffs.

The tie is made up of three pieces, two long strips and a loop for the knot. First sew up the two long strips and then pull the loop over both parts. The tie is sewn under the collar on one side, and on the other side it is fastened with a press stud.

This outfit for a girl doll includes an embroidered vest, long panties which can be tied at the waist, a petticoat with broderie anglaise trim, a pair of white hand knitted socks, a light blue dress with lace collar and a flowery pinafore. Instructions are not given for the socks.

Pattern pieces for doll's clothing

These pattern pieces are intended for reuse and should not be removed from this book. They have been reproduced to give the sizes needed to fit the clay and porcelain models in the Workshop section. Some indication of amounts of fabric have been given, but most of the garments can be made from scraps of suitable material.

Using tracing or grease-proof paper, draw round each section of the garment you are making and mark each piece clearly with the printed instructions. To enlarge or reduce the pattern, see the methods described on page 42.

Knitted or crochet garments are ideal for dolls and you should enquire about special patterns for toys in your local wool shop. As an alternative for a baby doll, choose a pattern for a layette and work the smallest size given in the instructions. A 40cm (16in) chest size would be suitable for a large doll, but the garment can also be reduced in size by using smaller sized needles, or hooks, to those recommended in the pattern.

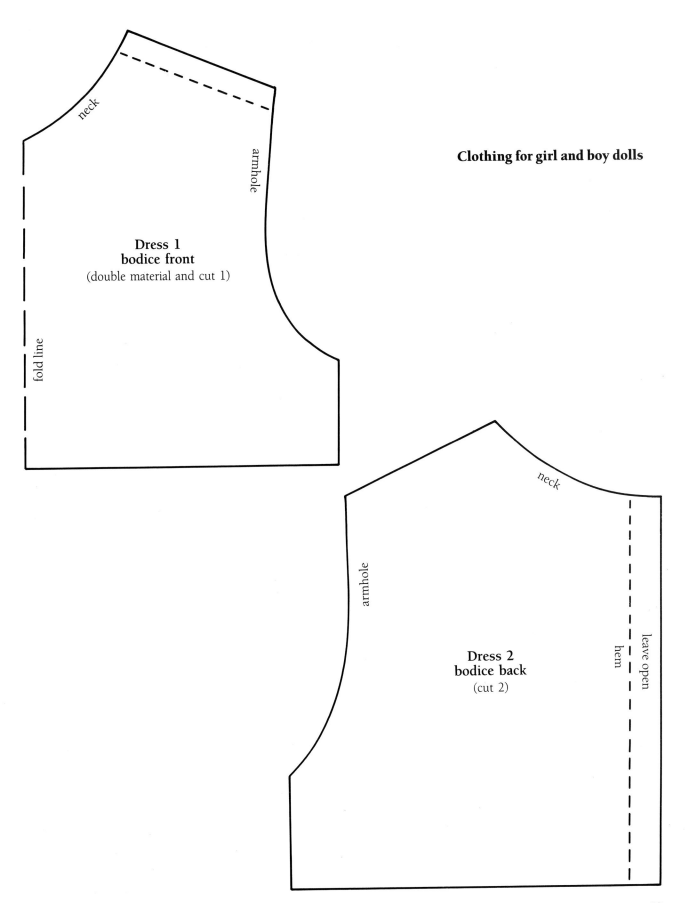

Clothing for girl and boy dolls

Dress 1
bodice front
(double material and cut 1)

neck

armhole

fold line

Dress 2
bodice back
(cut 2)

neck

armhole

leave open

hem

53

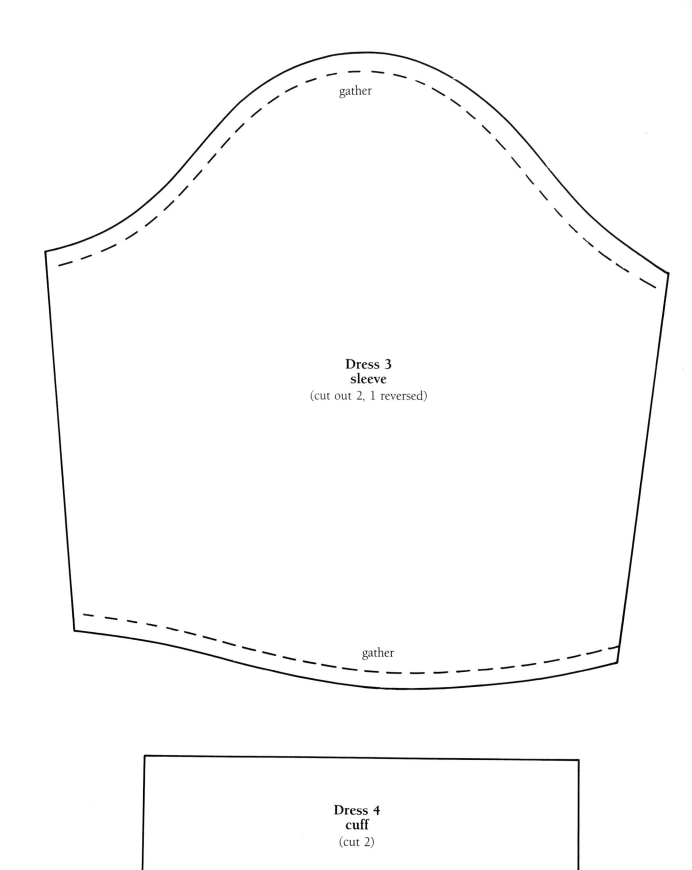

gather

Dress 3
sleeve
(cut out 2, 1 reversed)

gather

Dress 4
cuff
(cut 2)

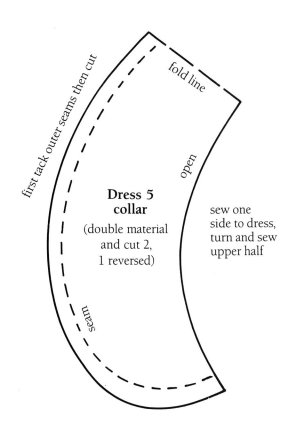

first tack outer seams then cut

fold line

open

**Dress 5
collar**

(double material
and cut 2,
1 reversed)

sew one
side to dress,
turn and sew
upper half

seam

**Dress 6
skirt**
cut piece 28 × 90cm (11 × 36in)

Petticoat
cut piece 24 × 80cm (9½ × 32in)

waistband
cut piece 31 × 4cm (12½ × 1½ in)
1.60m (60in) of lace for trimming

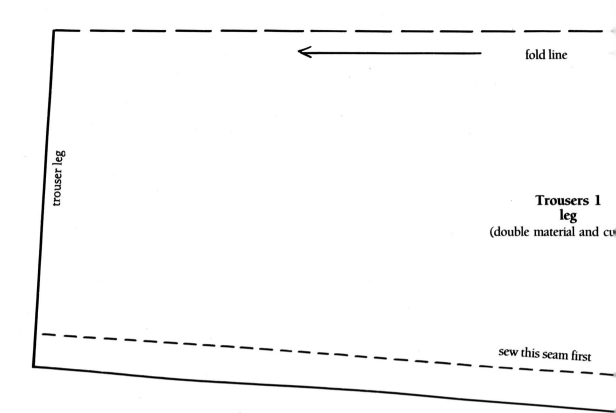

fold line

trouser leg

Trousers 1
leg
(double material and cu

sew this seam first

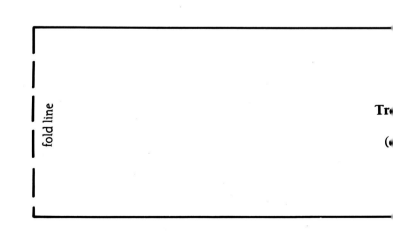

fold line

Tr

(

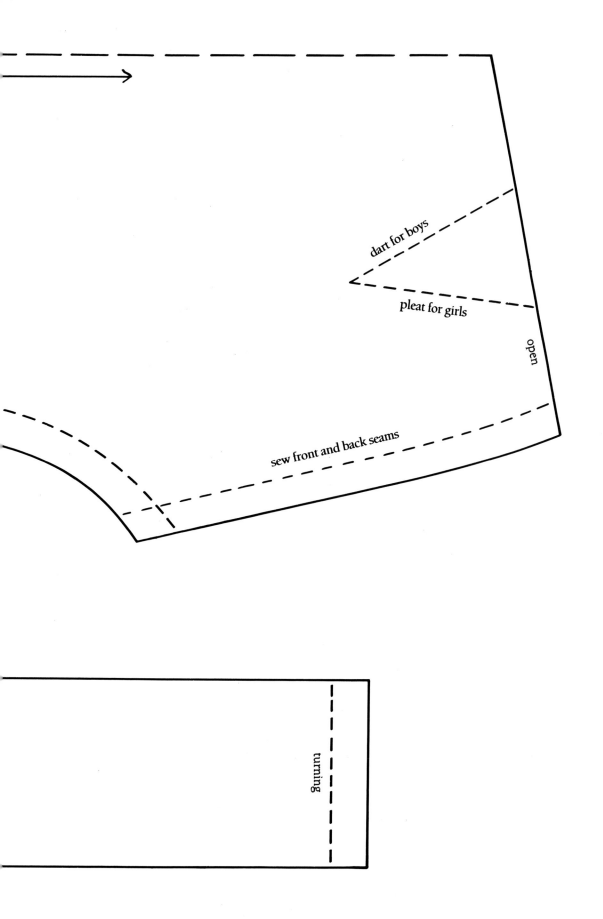

dart for boys

pleat for girls

open

sew front and back seams

turning

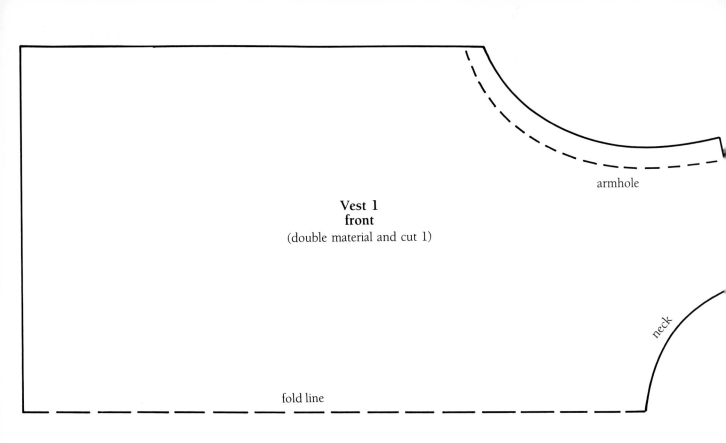

Vest 1
front
(double material and cut 1)

armhole

neck

fold line

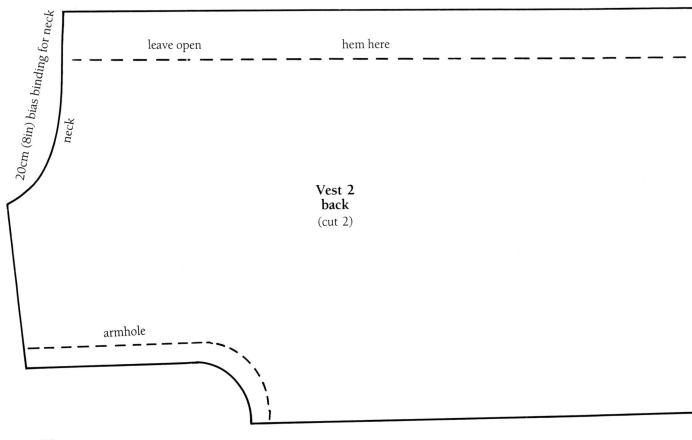

20cm (8in) bias binding for neck

leave open   hem here

neck

Vest 2
back
(cut 2)

armhole

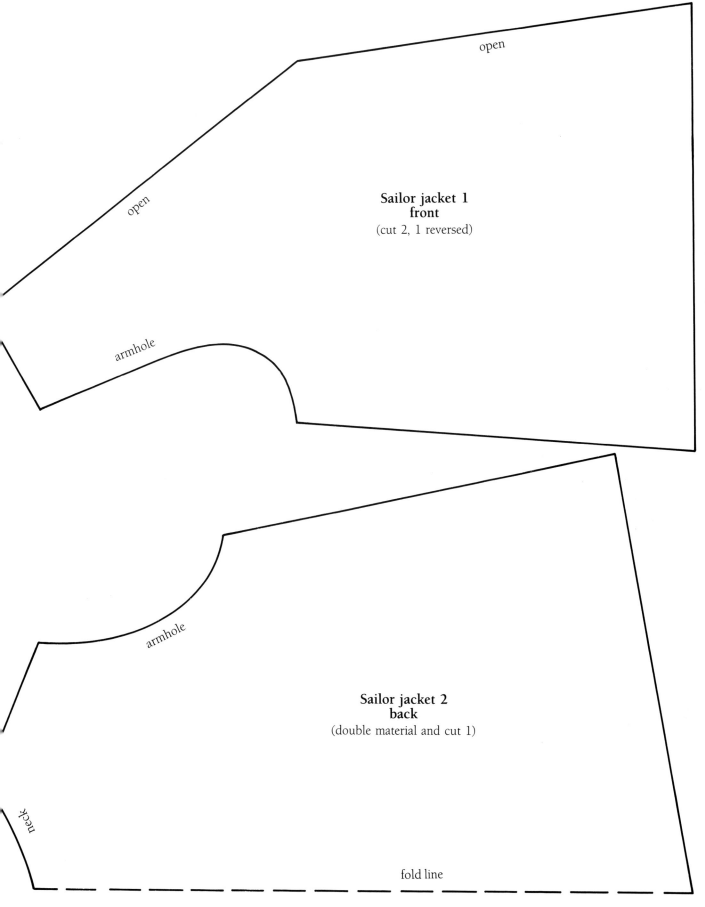

open

open

**Sailor jacket 1
front**
(cut 2, 1 reversed)

armhole

armhole

**Sailor jacket 2
back**
(double material and cut 1)

neck

fold line

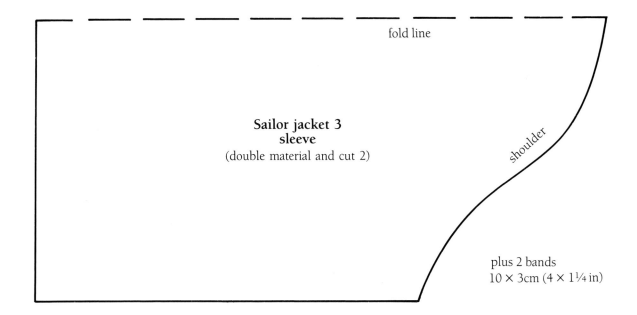

fold line

**Sailor jacket 3
sleeve**
(double material and cut 2)

shoulder

plus 2 bands
10 × 3cm (4 × 1¼ in)

**Sailor jacket 4
tie**
(double material and cut 2)

hem

fold line

fold line

**Sailor jacket 5
knot**
(double material and cut 2)

5 × 2½ cm (2 × 1in)

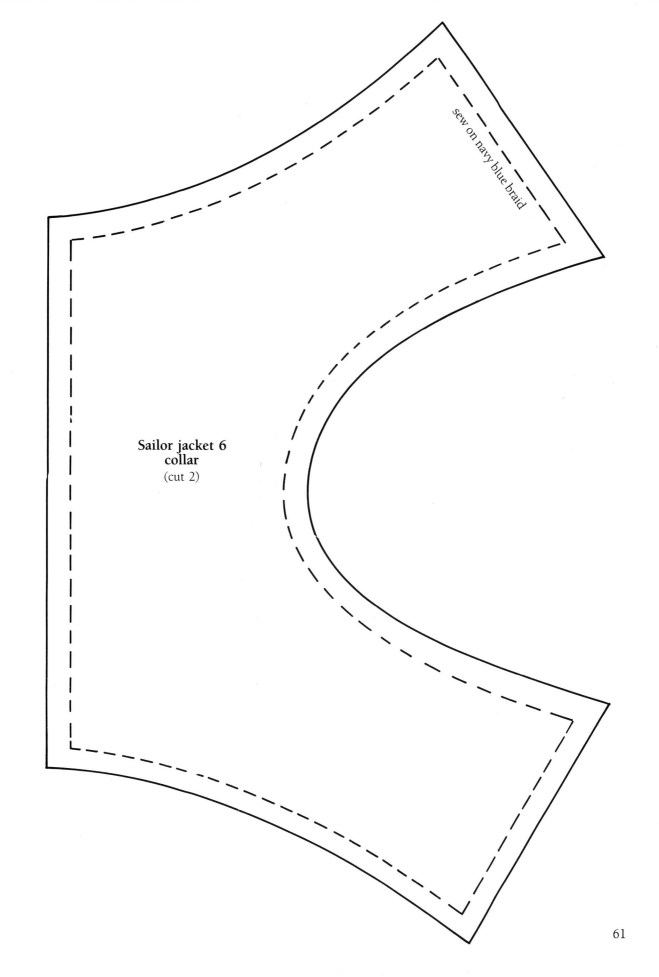

Sailor jacket 6
collar
(cut 2)

sew on navy blue braid

61

Gallery of dolls

You can make two porcelain dolls from the same mould and completely alter their appearance. Apart from the fact that when you are moulding and painting each doll you can change the expression and wig, clothes can also make the overall impression completely different. As you can see from the example of Alice and Philip, shown below, it is possible to make girl and boy dolls from the same mould.

Many good ideas come about by accident when you are experimenting. For example, when you are trying on wigs you may suddenly see exactly what clothes would suit the doll, and you should hang on to these first impressions. One of the nicest things about making dolls is that you can realize your own ideas, as the world of dolls is varied and colourful and everything is allowed, whatever you enjoy.

In this sense, harlequins and clowns also count as dolls. You should allow free rein to your imagination and bring cheerful, sad, comic or even mythical characters to life.

Sitting on the laundry basket are Simon and Henrietta, dressed in their casual clothes and ready to go out to play.

Henrietta has had enough of playing and has withdrawn for a while to be with her old teddy.

Simon is sitting happily in his high chair, waiting for his lunch which smells delicious.

Today, Julia is wearing her favourite hat to go with her dress.

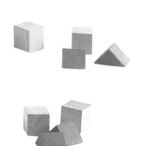

Rose and Melanie have built a house with their bricks.

Anne is wearing her bonnet and sitting in her basket chair, leafing through her favourite book.

Simon, whom we have already seen in modern dress on pages 64–5 is now dressed as baby Simone in a white hand embroidered linen dress, made from an old sheet and trimmed with crochet.

Victoria is shown in profile with a coiled plait. This porcelain doll is 60cm (24in) tall and her face was modelled on that of an eight-year-old girl. The soft mohair wig emphasizes her rosy complexion.

Today, Susan is wearing her best white Swiss-embroidered dress, because visitors are coming. Lots of little curls are escaping from her hair and framing her face.

Susan is wearing her blue dress with a flower-sprigged pinafore trimmed with broderie anglaise and she wears her hair in two neatly plaited coils. Her favourite teddy is sitting by the stove and wants to know whether there will soon be anything good to eat!

If only Jennifer knew what to do next! She cannot make up her mind whether she should play with her spinning-top or do her arithmetic homework.

The dark page-boy hair-style was the inspiration for this Asian-looking porcelain doll. The exotic clothes, the flower in the sash and the decorative fan, all emphasize the theme.

Alice has a blue bow in her hair and is wearing a pure silk dress. Anyone with a little sewing experience can make clothes from this beautiful material.

Felicity's face was modelled from the portrait of a teenage girl, and this porcelain doll is 65cm (26in) tall.

Till may well laugh in his joker's hat! He must be accompanied with his insignia – the owl and the mirror.

It was quite difficult to design the pointed headgear. It reaches from head to shoulders and has little bells at its points. You will find the pattern for the hat and also the shoes on pages 76–7.

Till has a bell on the point of each of his shoes and red stockings to go with them.

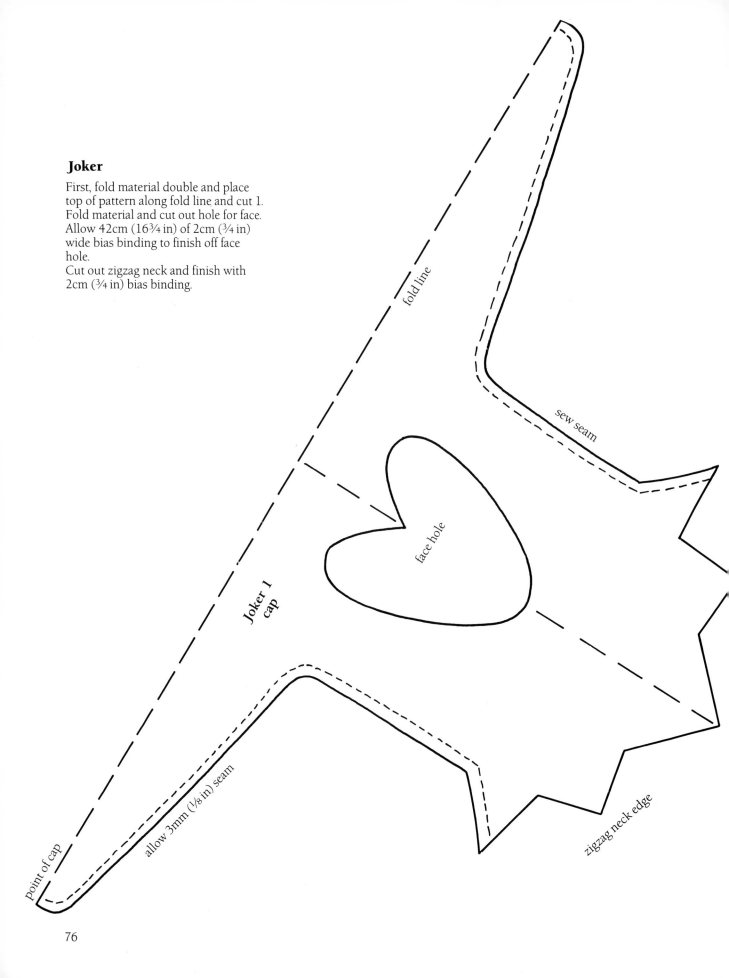

Joker

First, fold material double and place
top of pattern along fold line and cut 1.
Fold material and cut out hole for face.
Allow 42cm (16¾ in) of 2cm (¾ in)
wide bias binding to finish off face
hole.
Cut out zigzag neck and finish with
2cm (¾ in) bias binding.

fold line

sew seam

face hole

Joker 1
cap

allow 3mm (⅛ in) seam

point of cap

zigzag neck edge

Joker 2
left shoe

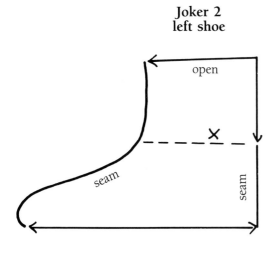

open

seam

×

seam

Joker 3
heel

open

dart

seam

seam

Joker 4
right shoe

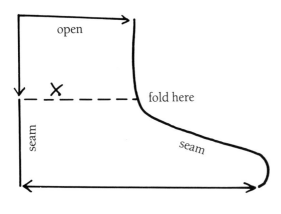

open

×

fold here

seam

seam

cut two of all pieces
3mm (⅛in) seam allowance included

× = fold here on the outside
and fasten with a stitch

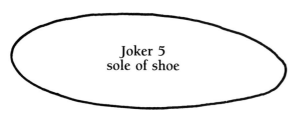

Joker 5
sole of shoe

inside foot

Mephistopheles creates a mysterious atmosphere. His head, hands and feet are modelled from clay and as can be seen from his clothes, a fanciful lace decoration is not solely reserved for women.

Mephistopheles' white face and lace bodice contrast with his mole-grey shirt and black collar. The grim mysterious expression is enhanced by the dark raised protuberant eyebrows and forehead. He does not wear a wig.

With fantasy figures, hands and feet should not be completely true to nature but may be modelled freely.

First published in Great Britain 1992 by
Search Press Limited,
Wellwood, North Farm Road,
Tunbridge Wells, Kent TN2 3DR

Reprinted 1998

Translated by Dinah Livingstone

Originally published in Germany by Falken-Verlag GmbH

The publishers and author would like to thank Mrs Luise Pflanz who kindly offered the
use of historical dolls' toys and accessories.

Cover picture: Photo-Design Hesselmann, Munich
Photos: Kulturhistorisches Bildarchiv Claus and Liselotte Hansmann, Munich: page 4–9;
Käthe-Kruse-Dolls Ltd, Donauwörth/Museum Den Helder: page 10 bottom;
Photo-Design Hesselmann, Munich: pages 1–3, page 8 top, pages 11–14, 23, 33, 35, 39,
62–75, 78–9
Fotoatelier Waltraud Münch-Mühlbacher, Ettendorf: pages 18–22, 24–31, 34, 38, 40–1,
46–9, 51
Drawings, Tables and Vignettes: Harmut Dietrich, Wiesbaden

ISBN 0 85532 721 9

*If readers have difficulty obtaining any of the materials or equipment in this book, please write
for further information to the publishers.*
Search Press Ltd, Wellwood, North Farm Road, Tunbridge Wells, Kent TN2 3DR, England.

Publisher's note
There is reference to sable hair and other animal hair
brushes in this book. It is the publisher's custom to
recommend synthetic materials as substitutes for
animal products wherever possible. There are now a
large number of brushes available made of artificial
fibres and they are just as satisfactory as those made of
natural fibres.

Composition by Genesis Typesetting, Rochester, Kent
Printed and bound in Malaysia by Times Offset